W9-BYU-030

WEATHER

NATURE *in* MOTION

WEATHER

NATURE *in* MOTION

Anne H. Oman

NATIONAL GEOGRAPHIC
Washington, D.C.

3 1800 00218 4519

CONTENTS

ON THE PRECEDING PAGES:
**Sugar maples in Vermont in summer, fall,
and winter weather. Opposite: Cumulus clouds
gather near the horizon, beneath cirrus clouds.**

A FORCE
OF NATURE

*"Everybody talks about the weather,
but nobody does anything about it."*
MARK TWAIN

It delivers bumper crops, but can also trigger famines. It spawns industries, but can devastate whole countries. It can get ships and planes to their destinations faster, but can also bring transportation to a standstill. It produces energy, but can also smash infrastructures and plunge cities into darkness and chaos.

What are we talking about?

The phenomenon that is perhaps the world's most persistent topic of conversation: the weather.

Most of the time, weather affects our daily lives in fairly routine ways. It dictates whether we bring an umbrella to work, whether we can plan a weekend picnic, whether we should pack our skis or our swimsuits. Weather can also change the way we feel—both physically and mentally. Many older people complain that damp weather makes their bones ache. And too many days without sunshine can give almost anyone a case of "the blues." But all too often, weather breaks out of its day-to-day routine and reminds us of its awesome power.

Seen from space, towers of clouds bring rain and thunder to southern Brazil. Clouds are an integral part of Earth's water cycle, returning moisture to the planet.

A summer thunderstorm also helped save Washington, D.C., from total destruction during the War of 1812 by quenching fires set by the British. A cold, snowy Russian winter helped defeat Napoleon's troops in 1812, contributing to the decline of his fortunes. And weather dealt the final blow three years later when a thunderstorm delayed the Battle of Waterloo by two hours, buying time for Prussian troops to come to the aid of faltering Wellington.

Even with the more advanced technology of modern times, weather remains a powerful factor in determining the course of war. A sudden wind, for example, blew poison gas launched by the Germans during World War I back onto their own lines, killing four regiments. In planning the D-Day invasion during World War II, Allied commanders took meteorological factors into full account. The invasion was timed so that the sea was calm enough to transport and land troops and the atmosphere clear enough for flight operations. When military meteorologists saw a window of opportunity—a ridge of high pressure moving across the English Channel—the "go" signal was given, and the Allies took a giant step toward victory.

Today's military commanders also work to make sure weather is on their side.

"We always have meteorologists assigned to major staffs, and all operations and plans have weather factored in," said Lieutenant Commander Nick Balise of the Defense Department's Central Command in Tampa, Florida, which runs the war in Iraq. "Cloud cover, for example, impacts flight operations. And early on in the Iraq war, when we were securing oil and gas platforms in the Gulf, it was crucial to know the sea state."

DEFINING WEATHER

What is this powerful force that can change history and influence our daily lives?

According to the American Meteorological Society, weather is "the state of the atmosphere, mainly with respect to its effect upon life and human activities at a particular time." Unlike climate, weather consists of short-term variations in the atmosphere—from minutes to weeks. No one ever asks, "How's the climate today?" The term "climate" usually refers to the average weather in a particular place or region over a much longer time frame, usually 30 years. In other words, "climate is what we expect—weather is what we get."

What causes these changes in the state of the atmosphere we refer to as weather?

Ancient and primitive peoples believed that favorable and unfavorable weather conditions were rewards and punishments from gods or supernatural forces. By placating the gods, they believed they could influence the weather.

The people of Lower Egypt, for example, believed that the god Set brought desert storms, and sought to appease him. The ancient Greeks often depicted Zeus, the most powerful god, with a thunderbolt. They believed he controlled weather, particularly thunderstorms. In *The Iliad,* Homer's epic poem, Zeus unleashed storms against his enemies. Ancient Chinese revered Yu, the god of soil, who harnessed rivers and tamed floods.

The Pueblo Indians of the southwestern United States staged elaborate ritual dances to bring on rain. The Aztecs believed their rain god Tlaloc, or "he who makes things sprout," lived high in the mountains, bestowing life-giving rain on the people below to grow maize and fruit. But Tlaloc could also be vengeful, sending destructive hurricanes and floods as punishments. To keep on Tlaloc's good side, the Aztecs built mountain-like temples and sometimes sacrificed humans to placate him.

The Zulus of Africa's Kalahari Desert worshipped a storm goddess named Inkanyamba, a giant winged snake. Inkanyamba wandered the sky, flying low and looking for her mate, who lived in water. If she saw anything that looked like water, she coiled down, bringing a tornado. As recently as 1998, a tornado in this region was attributed to Inkanyamba.

ROLE OF THE SUN

Today, scientists know what causes weather, and the players aren't gods but natural forces. The leading actor is the sun, and the theater is Earth's atmosphere, an envelope of air laden with moisture and bound to earth by gravity.

Jupiter, seen at top center in this painting by Francois Verdier, reigned over the Roman pantheon and was revered as the god of thunder and lightning and the sender of rain.

The sun's radiation filters through the atmosphere. Due to the tilt of the Earth, the sun's heat is unevenly distributed, with the areas near the Equator receiving the most solar radiation. The heated air rises and moves toward the Poles, and the cooled air moves back toward the Equator. These circulating air masses create differences in pressure and, thus, winds. But the air masses don't move in a straight north-south line. The pattern of atmospheric convection is complicated by the rotation of the Earth, which creates the Coriolis effect, named for a French mathematician. Due to the Coriolis effect, the flow of air turns toward the right in the Northern Hemisphere and toward the left in the Southern Hemisphere.

Differences in pressure combine with the Coriolis effect to move air masses. The leading edges of air masses of different temperatures are called "fronts"—possibly because the existence of distinct air masses was first discovered during World War I. Fronts are named for the air behind them. If the air behind the front is warmer than the air ahead of it, it is a "warm front." Because of their different temperatures, the air masses behind fronts don't mix easily. When a warm air mass and a cold air mass meet, the warm air rises above the cold air. The warm air cools and spreads, creating an area of low pressure, called a trough. If the air contains enough water vapor, the vapor may condense, forming clouds. That's why low pressure systems are often associated with cloudy, rainy weather. High pressure systems, or ridges, occur when air sinks toward the ground. The air dries as it descends, inhibiting cloud formation. That's why high pressure is generally associated with fair weather. Much of the "action" in weather—high winds, temperature changes, rising or falling

pressure—occurs along or near these fluid battle lines where air masses meet and clash.

Temperature, pressure, and precipitation are the basics of weather, but, of course, they aren't the whole picture. Landmasses, the seas, ocean temperatures, sunspots, mountains, industrial pollution, and many other factors play a role.

But all weather events—from heat waves to blizzards to hurricanes and tornadoes—can be better understood by looking at the system of cycles and forces set in motion in the Earth's atmosphere by the prime mover in weather: the sun.

CHANGING THE WEATHER

Other than understanding weather, can we do anything to counter its bad effects? Or was Mark Twain correct in saying "Everybody talks about the weather, but nobody does anything about it." ?

People have certainly tried to change weather—first by propitiating the weather gods and later by more scientific methods. One of the first efforts to use science to modify the weather was conducted by Dr. Vincent J. Schaefer at the General Electric Laboratory in Schenectady, New York, in the late 1940s. Known as the father of modern weather modification, Dr. Schaefer discovered that "seeding" clouds with various materials—such as salt crystals, silver iodide, or dry ice—could produce or increase rainfall. These materials form nuclei around which water vapor can condense.

Smog—fog laden with industrial pollutants—shrouds the U.S. East Coast. The burning of fossil fuels is changing the mix of greenhouse gases in the atmosphere and heating up the Earth, with potentially disastrous consequences.

Today, cloud seeding is used not only to increase rain, but to suppress hail. According to Dr. Terry Krauss, a cloud physicist who works for Weather Modification, Inc., his company has helped reduced hail damage in a defined area of Alberta, Canada, by about 50 percent.

Many thunderstorms produce hail because they are slow to make ice or make relatively few ice particles, he explained. That allows the ice to grow into large, damaging hailstones, which are too big to melt before they reach the ground.

"We seed the clouds with silver iodide. This is an ice nucleus. It begins the freezing process at a relatively warm temperature. For every liter of cloudy air, there's only one nucleus provided by nature," Dr. Krauss said in an interview. "Nature is very inefficient—that's why hail forms in clouds."

Dr. Krauss and his colleagues fly into the edges of a storm and drop lighted flares containing silver iodide, which fall through the clouds and cause the water vapor to freeze around its smoke particles. A second plane, with lighted flares attached to its wings, flies near the bottom of the clouds; the smoke from the flares is drawn up into the clouds. The water in the clouds freezes around the nuclei, and the frozen waterdrops melt on their way to Earth and fall as rain—not harmful hail.

IS THIS MESSING WITH MOTHER NATURE?

"We do it all the time," said Dr. Krauss. "We irrigate the desert. We use fertilizer and pesticides.... By reducing hail damage, there's an enormous opportunity for big benefits."

Weather modification has also been attempted—with less success—on hurricanes. In the 1960s, NOAA teamed with the U.S. Navy in a research effort known as Project Stormfury. The team seeded clouds just outside the eye of the hurricane wall with silver iodide, a substance that prompts supercooled water to freeze. The idea was that the freezing would take away some of the moist air that helps hurricanes grow. Although the effort seemed to mitigate two hurricanes—Beulah in 1963 and Debbie in 1969—no one really knew whether the hurricanes might have weakened on their own. And now,

To prevent hail from forming in thunderclouds (opposite), a small plane equipped with flares releases smoke into moisture-laden clouds, seeding them with silver iodide crystals (above).

ON THE FOLLOWING PAGES: **Baseball-size hail, remnants of a huge storm, lie strewn across a field near Lubbock, Texas. Each year, hail inflicts nearly $1 billion in damages to property and crops in the U.S.**

scientists believe that most hurricanes do not have enough supercooled water to respond to this treatment. In addition, hurricane seeding posed liability issues. If the seeding changed the course of a hurricane, could the people in the new hurricane path sue for the damages to their property caused by the storm?

FOREWARNED IS FOREARMED

Although some weather modification is still being tried, most meteorologists believe that the best weapon against bad weather is accurate forecasting.

"Forecasts are getting better and better," Senior Meteorologist Douglas Le Comte of the National Weather Service said in an interview. "People can plan—they can take themselves out of bad weather. And there's a real economic benefit to having good forecasting."

According to the World Meteorological Organization, national weather services that provide forecasts to their citizens contribute an estimated $20 to $40 billion a year to their national economies. A study by the U.S. National Weather Service showed that the aviation industry alone saves nearly half a billion dollars a year from the forecasting services it receives.

Forecasting has come a long way since the days when the only available aids were folk adages such as "The daisy shuts its eye before rain," and "Cats scratch a post before wind." Benjamin Franklin, who may have been the first American weather forecaster, crammed his *Poor Richard's Almanack* with inspirational maxims urging thrift and industry as well as forecasts based partly on his own observations made by flying kites in thunderstorms and chasing storms on horseback. In 1818, the *Farmers' Almanac* began publication. Still published every year, the almanac is crammed with gardening tips, astrology, homespun philosophy—and weather forecasts. According to the publishers, "We don't divine the weather by counting onion layers, measuring wooly-bear bands, or tabulating the acorns that squirrels sock away—although such phenomena may well be indicators of

Almanacs about the weather have long been popular. The *Old Farmer's Almanac* (bottom) has been in publication for more than 200 years, and Benjamin Franklin's *Poor Richard's Almanack* (top) ran for some 25 years.

upcoming weather." Instead, the *Almanac* uses a secret formula devised by its founder, Robert B. Thomas, ca 1792. The formula is based on sunspots, sun cycles, and the study of prevailing weather patterns.

Today, government and commercial weather services have an impressive array of scientific forecasting tools. Hydrogen-filled balloons called radiosondes measure temperature, humidity, and pressure in the atmosphere and radio them back to weather stations on Earth. Satellites track weather systems and transmit pictures. Buoys relay ocean and air temperatures. Commercial airplanes transmit weather observations every five minutes, and data from ships and automated weather stations around the world also goes into the mix.

In the United States, in addition to all the high-tech inputs, a network of unpaid volunteers also records and transmits weather information.

Robert Leffler, a self-described "weather weenie," is one of these 11,000 volunteers. "We're the folks who for over a hundred years have collected the vast bulk of information on the nation's climate and weather," he told me. "We take observations where you live,

Orbiting 438 miles above Earth, the Aura satellite is equipped with sensors that monitor ozone and measure emissions. The data collected helps scientists assess air quality and determine how Earth's climate is changing.

work, and grow your food. Not a lot of people live in airports."

Leffler's backyard in Damascus, Maryland, contains weather-watching equipment provided and maintained by the National Weather Service: a rain gauge, which "looks like a big juice can;" a temperature sensor with a beehive-like radiation shield; and a stake in the ground to measure total snow accumulation. To measure how much snow falls in a single day, Leffler uses a rectangular white board that measures about 18 by 24 inches.

"You measure snowfall from the board, because the ground is uneven," he explained. Observers are instructed to put snowboards out at the beginning of the season and to mark their location with an indicator such as a flag so they can be found easily after a snowfall. The boards should be placed in an open location—not under trees or obstructions or on the north side of structures.

Every 24 hours, Leffler records the day's maximum and minimum temperatures and measures the liquid in the rain gauge.

"You want the liquid precipitation equivalent," he explained. "The rain gauge collects hail, sleet, and snow as well as rain. What most volunteers do is pour in a measured

WANT TO BE A WEATHER OBSERVER?

....

National Weather Service Forecast Offices recruit volunteers to report local weather conditions. Volunteers, called Cooperative Observers, receive training and equipment. Requirements include:

■ *Dedication to public service*

■ *Attention to detail*

■ *Ability to learn and perform daily duties*

■ *Willingness to have equipment placed on your property, and willingness to allow at least one visit per year by a National Weather Service representative.*

Ownership of a personal computer and internet access are helpful but not mandatory.

For more information and to find out whether there are openings in your area, go to www.nws.noaa.gov/om/coop/indes.htm.

Battling the elements in Kansas, researchers studying severe weather launch weather balloons laden with sensors into a thunderstorm. The balloons collect data on temperature, humidity, pressure, wind direction, and electric fields.

amount of hot water. When you take the measured amount out, you have the liquid precipitation equivalent."

He transmits the information to the local office of the National Weather Service, along with a notation on any special phenomena, such as damaging winds or hail.

Weather observations from human observers and high-tech sources are fed into computers, which use the data to create maps showing where the air masses and fronts are and where they are heading. Armed with these maps, National Weather Service meteorologists use their knowledge about weather patterns—as well as computer models—to predict the weather. They issue guidance forecasts to 120 local weather offices around the country, which issue warnings and make specific forecasts for their locales.

"In medical terminology, we're the specialists, and the local forecasters are the G.P.s," explained National Weather Service meteorologist Edwin J. Danaher.

"They're looking at the hemisphere—we're looking at the local level," said meteorologist David Manning of the Baltimore-Washington Forecast Office in Sterling, Virginia. In a large field outside the forecast office, radar antennas scanned the skies. Inside,

ON THE FOLLOWING PAGES: **Scientists predict that much of the globe (shown in yellow, orange, and red) will experience hotter nights, and worse heat waves, by the 22nd century unless greenhouse gases are curtailed.**

HOTSPOTS

The places around the world projected to experience hotter nights—and more severe heat waves—appear in red (hottest), orange, and yellow. Scientists at the National Center for Atmospheric Research predict that, unless greenhouse gases are curtailed, these places will see worse heat waves by the end of the 21st century.

There is no standard definition of "heat wave," but one simple definition can be "the three worst nights of the summer," that is, the three highest consecutive readings of daily minimum temperature (daily minimum temperature is recorded at night). Then we may ask how much worse will the three worst nights become, on average, in a future with no curbing of greenhouse gas emissions. The answer is in this figure. At each point on the map the color corresponds to a value in degrees Celsius (red is hottest). This value is the expected magnitude of the warming during the three worst nights of the summer, in the climate of the end of the 21st century (its last two decades, to be precise). For example, the Mediterranean basin will experience the three hottest nights of the summer becoming warmer still, by on average 3 to 4 degrees Celsius with respect to what is observed currently in the region. Similarly, in the West and Southwest of the

U.S. the three worst nights of the summer will be warmer by on average 2.5 to 3.5 degrees Celsius.

These results were obtained by a climate model simulation, under a scenario of future anthropogenic emissions called "business as usual." Under this scenario, as the name suggests, no major changes in terms of mitigation policy are expected, and the rate of greenhouse gas emissions is projected to remain constant at the current levels.

The climate model used is the PCM (Parallel Climate Model), developed as a joint venture between NCAR (the National Center for Atmospheric Research, funded by NSF) and the Department of Energy.

forecasters and technicians sat in front of computer screens displaying images of their sprawling forecast area, comprised of most of two states plus the District of Columbia. Superimposed on the maps were temperature readings, river levels, wind directions, precipitation, and other weather indicators—some relayed from automated weather stations and some reported by cooperative weather observers who are, in Mr. Manning's words, "beyond invaluable."

"We launch weather balloons twice a day," said Mr. Manning. "We feed data to the national office, and they run computer models. We look at the full observational data set—radar, satellites, reports from aircraft—and we also look at model guidance. We're not likely to take the computer model verbatim."

"You have to use your experience, knowledge, and insights to decide when you can trust the model and when its output may not be real," said forecaster Roger Smith, who is at the short-term desk, preparing the forecast for the next two 12-hour periods. "Even though we have a lot of technology, forecasting is still an art. Some people have a knack, a sense that the atmosphere is going to change."

TOWARD BETTER FORECASTS

Weather officials point out that the accuracy of forecasting has improved tremendously in recent years.

"Accuracy is going up for all forecasts—short, medium, and long range," said Dr. Louis W. Uccellini, Director of the National Centers for Environmental Prediction. "Accuracy is greater than 90 to 95 percent for 24 hours. As you get out to day seven, accuracy drops off. For general weather forecasts at day seven, accuracy is about 60 percent. In the early 1970s, we could only issue winter storm warnings 12 hours in advance. Today, we can forecast the probability of heavy snow events five to six days in advance and issue warnings 24 hours in advance. Fifteen years ago, we couldn't touch a major snowstorm before day two. The 1993 superstorm we forecast five days in advance."

To further improve accuracy, the National Weather Service is working on improving both technology and observation capability.

"We're not only improving individual numerical models, but we're creating ensembles," said Dr. Uccellini. "Ensemble forecasting is a collection of forecasts generated by models—it gives us an envelope of solutions."

Think of a symphony orchestra, with all the musicians playing together. If one violinist makes a mistake, it doesn't necessarily ruin the whole concert—the other musicians drown out the error.

"The atmosphere and the ocean are fluids, and fluids

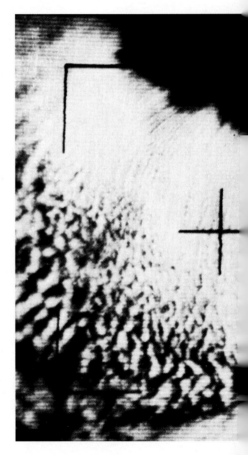

can be defined with equations," he continued. "It's Newtonian: f = ma. Force equals mass times acceleration. You're trying to compute the 'a.' Atmosphere can be set up as an initial value problem. You define the parameters and see what happens when you step ahead in time. Atmosphere is a continuum, but the models break it into cubes. One cube might include all the atmosphere between Washington and Baltimore, but it could be raining in Baltimore and not here. So you take a sample at one point that might not be accurate at another point. Discretization introduces errors…. We're getting data from many sources—satellites, airplanes. We have to interpolate and get all that information onto a grid. In doing so, we're bound to introduce errors."

To improve the accuracy of the forecasts, the meteorologists run multiple models and change some of the inputs.

"What if we made Canada cooler or raised the temperature over California four degrees and ran the model 40 times?" asked Dr. Uccellini. "If all 40 say the same thing, you can have confidence in the forecast. If 20 say there will be a storm, and 20 don't, you can quantify and give people a level of certainty. If you're in charge of the schools and I can tell you with 90 percent certainty there will be a snowstorm tomorrow, you might want to cancel school. If it's a 30 percent chance, you might want to wait until the morning to make a decision."

Images from 1966 (left) and 2001 (right) show how technology has improved since the first weather satellite was launched in 1960. Today's satellites have higher resolution and also relay data on temperature and moisture.

With ensemble forecasting, meteorologists can help counter a powerful force: chaos.

Mathematician and meteorologist Edward Lorenz discovered chaos theory—the idea that the accuracy of the forecast in an inherently chaotic system such as weather depends on the precision of the original inputs—in 1963. While conducting computer experiments at M.I.T., he found that a slight error in initial measurements could lead to big mistakes down the line. In Lorenz's classic illustration of chaos theory, a butterfly flapping its wings in Brazil could, in theory, start a chain reaction resulting in a tornado in Texas.

To explain, Dr. Uccellini waved his arms up and down.

"Me moving my arms creates an eddy here in this room," he said. "If that eddy were

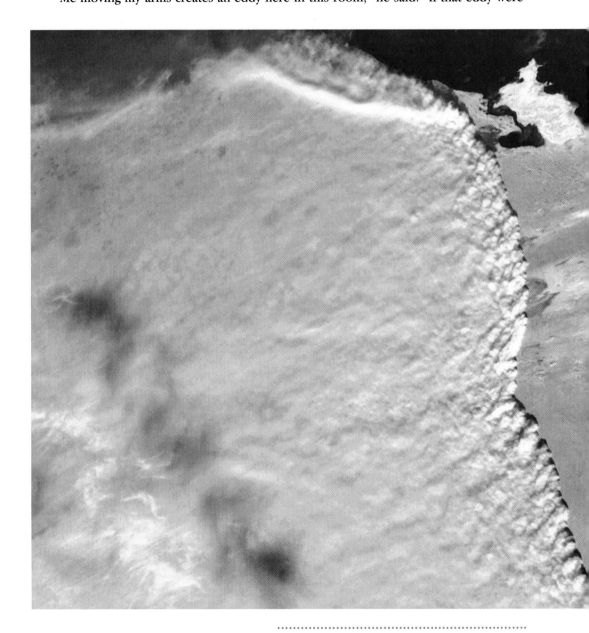

Sweeping over Qatar, a massive sandstorm races toward Saudi Arabia in this photograph taken from the International Space Station on February 15, 2004. Low pressure in the upper atmosphere unloosed the strong winds.

to be introduced into a discretized grid in a model, we'd be introducing an error that could keep being amplified.... You can never eliminate errors. The question is, Will the error that you introduce grow so big it will overwhelm the accuracy of the forecast?"

Although the accuracy of weather forecasts is improving—and is expected to improve significantly in the future—most meteorologists don't expect to eliminate chaos and unexpected weather events entirely.

"There's a lot of randomness," says meteorologist Douglas Le Comte of NOAA's Climate Prediction Center. "Sometimes the atmosphere just does what it feels like doing,"

And that's one reason weather is such a fascinating subject.

TEMPERATURE, HEAT WAVES, AND COLD SNAPS

"As long as the earth endures, cold and heat,
seedtime and harvest, summer and winter, day and night shall not cease."
GENESIS

The sun lights the sky, but less than half of its radiant energy reaches Earth as heat. As the Earth spins on its axis at an angle of 23.4 degrees, the sun's rays shine most directly on places nearest the Equator; near the Poles, the sun's rays hit the Earth at smaller angles, resulting in colder climates. Different areas of the Earth face the sun at different times of the year, creating seasons: summer, fall, winter, and spring. When the North Pole is angled toward the sun – in the Northern Hemisphere's summer – more of the sun's rays hit the northern parts of the globe, making longer, warmer days. When the North Pole is angled away from the sun, the Northern Hemisphere experiences winter. In spring and fall, both Poles are equidistant from the sun.

Hot or cold climates rarely make news. But unusual spikes or dips in the thermometer that catch people unprepared for extreme heat or cold generate alarm, and often, tragedy. The August 2003 heat wave in normally temperate northern Europe is a good example.

Tourists bask in the setting sun on Australia's Cable Beach. The sun's radiant energy unevenly heats the Earth. Places near the Equator, which get direct rays, are hottest.

Temperatures soared, peaking at 106°F in Seville, 104°F in Madrid, 100°F in Paris, as Europe baked and fried in the worst heat wave ever recorded, by some estimates the hottest summer since 1500. According to the Associated Press, deaths from the heat wave exceeded 19,000—most of them in France, where many elderly people could not survive in their sweltering apartments. With much of France enjoying the traditional August vacation, many of the dead lay unclaimed as notification proved difficult. In Paris, morticians used a refrigerated warehouse outside the city to store bodies, since there wasn't enough space in their own facilities. French gravediggers were called back to work on a national holiday—August 15—to bury the dead. By September, 66 bodies were still unclaimed.

Although other countries suffered fewer deaths, the effects of the heat wave were felt all over Europe. In Spain, experts warned of a proliferation of jellyfish as the Mediterranean heated up. In Portugal, forest fires inflicted heavy damage. Glaciers melted in the Alps, causing avalanches and flash floods. Nuclear power plants in Germany cut production to avoid overheating water in the cooling towers that empty into rivers. British trains ran slower, for fear of melting tracks.

Relief arrived with a cold front on August 17, causing severe thunderstorms but returning temperatures to normal range.

WHAT CAUSED THE HEAT WAVE?

Generally, heat waves are caused by a strong ridge of high pressure in the upper atmosphere that becomes nearly stationary over a

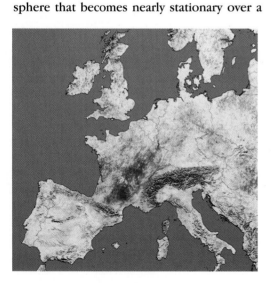

A blanket of red on this satellite image (left) marks where temperatures averaged 18 degrees hotter than normal during Europe's sizzling summer of 2003. A Paris physician (above) uses ice to cool a patient suffering from hyperthermia.

given area. In this case, the high pressure ridge blocked cool air from blowing in off the Atlantic Ocean. But some experts have raised the possibility that the 2003 heat wave was the result of global warming, an overall rise in average temperatures worldwide.

The summer of 2003 was the hottest in the last five centuries, according to researchers from the University of Bern, Switzerland. Scientists analyzed written records, soil cores, and tree rings dating back to 1500, and found that average annual temperatures in Europe from 1973 through 2002 were the warmest in 500 years. They published their findings in the journal *Science.* The scientists did not, however, draw any conclusions about whether the warming trend was caused by greenhouse gases and the burning of fossil fuels.

"You can't blame an individual heat wave on global warming," said Douglas Le Comte of the National Weather Service's Climate Prediction Center. "You have to separate weather events from long-term climate change."

But in a computer modeling study published in the journal *Science* on August 13, 2004, scientists Gerald Meehl and Claudia Tebaldi of the National Center for Atmospheric Research in Boulder, Colorado, predict that heat waves in Paris, Chicago, and elsewhere in Europe and the United States will become more frequent, more intense, and longer lasting in the 21st century due to increasing greenhouse gases.

Increasing carbon dioxide in the atmosphere, the scientists found, will intensify the pattern observed during heat waves in Europe and North America: changes in atmospheric pressure that produce clear skies and prolonged high temperatures. The scientists predict that heat waves in the western and southern United States and the Mediterranean region of Europe will become more severe because minimum nighttime temperatures will rise by an average of close to 5°C, depriving people of nighttime cooling. The average annual number of heat waves in the Chicago area will increase by 25 percent, and the number in Paris will increase by 31 percent.

Another study, conducted by British scientists and published in the journal *Nature* on December 2, 2004, estimated that human-induced increases in greenhouse gases and other pollutants has at least doubled the risk of heat waves of the magnitude of the European heat wave of 2003.

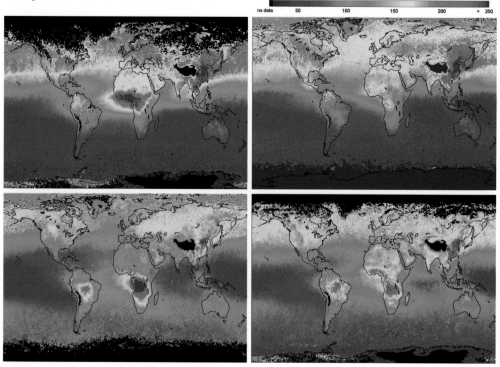

A series of color-coded satellite images reveal the concentration and distribution of carbon monoxide, a pollutant that comes from automobile emissions and fire activity (such as slash and burn), in the atmosphere.

ON THE OPPOSITE PAGE: Scientists believe industrial pollution and automobile emissions are changing the mix of greenhouse gases in the atmosphere, trapping more heat and warming the globe.

According to the National Oceanic and Atmospheric Administration (NOAA), global surface temperatures have increased about 0.4°F over the past 25 years, although the warming has not been uniform over all parts of the globe. Some of this warming may be due to natural variability—such as changes in the sun's energy output or in the Earth's orbit. But most scientists believe that an intensified "greenhouse effect" is the prime player in global warming, and that human activity—particularly the burning of fossil fuels—plays a role. The Intergovernmental Panel on Climate Change concluded that "the balance of evidence suggests that there is a discernible human influence on global climate."

Roughly 2 percent of the Earth's atmosphere consists of greenhouse gases—mainly water vapor and carbon dioxide. These gases act as a greenhouse—trapping part of the Earth's heat and preventing it from escaping into space. Without this natural greenhouse effect, the temperature would be too cold to support life as we know it—about 0°F, on average. But in the past 40 years or so, scientists have noted a change in the makeup of greenhouses gases. Water vapor is still the dominant component, but the percentage of carbon dioxide, which is more effective at trapping heat than water vapor, is growing. Carbon dioxide is CONTINUED ON PAGE 46

THE AIR IS SO THICK YOU COULD CUT IT WITH A KNIFE.

Wrong!
You often hear such plaints on humid days, but meteorologically speaking, they couldn't be farther from the truth. In fact, humid air is lighter not heavier than dry air. Isaac Newton was the first scientist to recognize this concept, in his 1717 second edition of Opticks. *Water vapor molecules actually weigh less than molecules of air. So if you replace nitrogen and oxygen molecules with water molecules, the air is lighter.*

ON PAGES 42-43: **Slash and burn agricultural practices promote global warming in two ways: by adding carbon dioxide to greenhouse gases and by stripping the earth of shade-giving plants and trees.**

ON PAGES 44-45: **The nearly 4,000 firefly-like dots in this satellite image represent fires burning in central Africa in May 2004, most probably set to clear land for farming.**

TIPS FOR COPING WITH EXTREME HEAT

The U.S. Centers for Disease Control offers the following advice on how to prevent heat-related illness:

- Stay indoors, preferably in an air conditioned place. If your home is not air-conditioned, go to a shopping mall or public library or other air-conditioned place for a few hours. Ask your local health department if there are any heat-related shelters in your area.
- Drink more nonalcoholic fluids, but avoid drinks that contain caffeine or large amounts of sugar. Also, avoid very cold drinks.
- Take cool showers or baths.
- Wear lightweight, light-colored, loose-fitting clothing; a wide-brimmed hat; sunglasses; and sunscreen.
- Never leave a person or animal in a closed, parked vehicle.
- Check regularly on infants and young children, people 65 or older, and mentally or physically ill people, especially those with heart disease or high blood pressure.
- Limit outdoor activity to morning or evening.
- Cut down on exercise.
- Rest often in shady areas.

Source: NOAA

produced by the burning of fossil fuels and by burning forests. This increase in heat-trapping greenhouse gases is being amplified by feedback effects—such as a decrease in snow cover and sea ice and an increase in atmospheric water vapor.

Whatever its causes, the European heat wave of 2003 was exacerbated by nonmeteorological factors: few homes in northern Europe are equipped with air conditioners; August is the traditional vacation month and many elderly were left without a support group of relatives; hospitals and emergency rooms were short staffed due to the vacation as well. Many people blamed the government for not taking emergency measures promptly.

HISTORIC HEAT WAVES

Heat waves are nothing new. Eastern Europe, Scandinavia, and Russia experienced sweltering heat in the summer of 1757—the hottest summer on record until 2003. In July 1901, the midwestern United States baked under record temperatures, and an estimated 9,500 people died of

Black and white and hot all over, a giant panda hugs a block of ice during a heat wave in Chengdu, China (above). At right, a rickshaw driver hauls fans through the streets of New Delhi, India, in May 1994, when the thermometer hit 111°F.

heat-related causes. From August 31 to September 7, 1955, Los Angeles endured eight days of 100°F-plus temperatures that triggered nearly 1,000 deaths. 1980 saw a heat wave in the eastern and midwestern United States that killed an estimated 1,700 people and did more than $15 billion in economic damage. A 1995 heat wave hit several midwestern cities, including Chicago, where 716 people died—many of them elderly residents who were afraid to go out or even open windows for fear of crime. (In contrast, people slept on the banks of Lake Michigan in earlier heat waves). And in India, some 4,000 people died of heat-related causes in a 1998 heat wave that saw thermometers rise to 123°F. One of the most poignant deaths was that of a 30-year-old bridegroom who died of heat-related causes an hour after his wedding. Arjun Lande had walked around distributing wedding invitations to friends and relatives in the extreme heat. He complained of ill health on his wedding day, and collapsed soon after the cere- mony. Admitted to a nearby hospital, he died before medical care could be administered.

"Heat waves kill with silence," says Jim Hoke of the National Weather Service. "Intense heat can creep up on its victims, because it doesn't have the loud, crash and bang of a hurricane or tornado. Its average death toll, however, is much worse."

MEAN HEAT INDEX

As with most adverse weather events, the best way to cope with a heat wave is to be warned and prepared. The National Weather Service has developed a Mean Heat Index designed to give a big picture of how the heat may affect people. Instead of just predicting the high and low temperatures for the day, the Mean Heat Index number is an average of temperatures during the hottest and coolest part of the day. A Mean Heat Index high- er than 85 degrees is considered dangerous, according to the National Weather Service, because it may indicate that night- time temperatures haven't cooled.

"Heat waves often turn fatal when the nighttime tempera- ture doesn't drop very much from a high daytime tempera- ture," explained Jim Hoke. "The Mean Heat Index captures this potentially serious condition by including data from what should be a cooler portion of the day, and factoring that in to give a 'big picture' of the day's temperatures, not just the day's high."

The National Weather Service's Hydrometeorological Prediction Center puts out daily color-coded maps indicating the temperatures the Mean Heat Index is expected to reach in vari- ous regions of the United States. In addition, local predictions are sent out to 90 cities.

At the opposite end of the thermometer, cold temperatures can also wreak havoc in people's lives, as they did in February 1899 in what has been called the "mother of all cold waves."

In early February, an Arctic blast locked two-thirds of the United States in a frigid embrace, setting record cold temperatures that still stand in many cases. On February 10, the

Deep snow blocks all traffic in New York City's Harlem neighborhood during the "mother of all cold waves" in February 1899. The Arctic blast gripped the entire Eastern seaboard in a frigid embrace.

ON THE FOLLOWING PAGES: Horse-drawn carts line up to dump snow in the Hudson River during the cold wave of 1899, which piled more than a foot of snow on New York City.

temperature plunged to minus 20°F in Pittsburgh, minus 16°F in Cleveland. The next day, the nation's capital experienced its coldest temperature ever recorded, minus 15°F. Tallahassee, Florida, reported a reading of minus 2°F. Ice jams on the Ohio, James, Tennessee, and Cumberland Rivers caused widespread flooding, and ports in the Great Lakes froze. The Mississippi River, where not frozen solid, was filled with large masses of floating ice. On February 17, some of these floating ice islands reached New Orleans—to the amazement of residents who had never seen ice—and flowed into the Gulf of Mexico. In the meantime, a powerful snowstorm worked its way up the East Coast, burying Philadelphia, New Jersey, New York City, and much of New England under three feet of snow. In a sense, the areas that got the snow were the lucky ones: In Chicago, the lack of snow allowed the freeze to penetrate deep into the ground, damaging water, gas, and service pipes.

Unlike heat waves, cold snaps generally don't kill people. Although extreme cold can be at least as lethal as extreme heat, people usually die from long-term or chronic

Like jagged chunks of glass, ice piles up on the shores of Mackinac Island, in Michigan's Lake Huron. Extreme cold waves have stopped shipping and closed ports on the Great Lakes, bringing commerce to a halt.

Wind Chill Index

Temperature

Wind (mph) Calm	40	35	30	25	20	15	10	5	0	-5	-10	-15	-20	-25	-30	-35	-40	-45
5	36	31	25	19	13	7	1	-5	-11	-16	-22	-28	-34	-40	-46	-52	-57	-63
10	34	27	21	15	9	3	-4	-10	-16	-22	-28	-35	-41	-47	-53	-59	-66	-72
15	32	25	19	13	6	0	-7	-13	-19	-26	-32	-39	-45	-51	-58	-64	-71	-77
20	30	24	17	11	4	-2	-9	-15	-22	-29	-35	-42	-48	-55	-61	-68	-74	-81
25	29	23	16	9	3	-4	-11	-17	-24	-31	-37	-44	-51	-58	-64	-71	-78	-84
30	28	22	15	8	1	-5	-12	-19	-26	-33	-39	-46	-53	-60	-67	-73	-80	-87
35	28	21	14	7	0	-7	-14	-21	-27	-34	-41	-48	-55	-62	-69	-76	-82	-89
40	27	20	13	6	-1	-8	-15	-22	-29	-36	-43	-50	-57	-64	-71	-78	-84	-91
45	26	19	12	5	-2	-9	-16	-23	-30	-37	-44	-51	-58	-65	-72	-79	-86	-93
50	26	19	12	4	-2	-10	-17	-24	-31	-38	-45	-52	-60	-67	-74	-81	-88	-95
55	25	18	11	4	-3	-11	-18	-25	-32	-39	-46	-54	-61	-68	-75	-82	-89	-97
60	25	17	10	3	-4	-11	-19	-26	-33	-40	-48	-55	-62	-69	-76	-84	-91	-98

30 Minutes

10 Minutes

5 Minutes

exposure to cold rather than short cold snaps. But economic damages are staggering. A Christmas cold snap in 1983 destroyed $1 billion worth of citrus fruit in Florida. A cold wave in the winter of 1976-77 ran up a bill of $3.8 billion in increased energy costs.

WHAT CAUSES COLD WAVES?

Most cold waves happen when the polar jet stream, an undulating river of powerful winds high in the atmosphere that usually sits above the U.S.-Canadian border, dives south. In such instances, the polar jet stream can merge with the subtropical jet stream to form one bigger, more powerful river. In the 1899 cold wave, for example, meteorologists think the combined jet stream went as far south as Mexico's Yucatán Peninsula. When the two jet streams are not merged, the existence of the subtropical jet can keep colder air out of the southern and middle Atlantic states and bring warmer weather.

Back in 1899, nobody mentioned the "wind chill temperature;" today, meteorologists report it regularly. Standard temperature readings measure the temperature of the air close to Earth, but do not necessarily tell you how cold you're going to be when you get outside. A human being loses body heat when exposed to cold air, and wind accelerates this heat loss. The greater the wind speed, the faster you lose heat.

How cold does it feel? You can use the National Weather Service Wind Chill Temperature Index to figure out how cold the temperature and wind combined are making your body feel and whether or not you're in danger of frostbite. For example, if the thermometer reads 25°F, and the wind is blowing at 20 miles an hour, the wind chill temperature is 11°F, and you don't have to worry about frostbite. But if the thermometer dips to 5°F and the winds rev up to 30 miles an hour, the wind chill temperature is minus 19°F and 30 minutes of outdoor exposure could result in frostbite.

EL NIÑO AND LA NIÑA

When El Niño brings warmer-than-usual temperatures to ocean waters off the west coast of South America, it also brings temperature changes to the continental United States. These changes are most marked during the winter. During El Niño years—about every two to seven years—the north-central States usually experience warmer-than-usual winters, while the Southeast and the Southwest see colder-than-normal temperatures.

La Niña—the opposite of El Niño—is characterized by colder-than-usual ocean temperatures in the eastern Pacific off the coasts of Peru and Chile. Among other effects, La Niña changes the pattern of tropical rainfall from Indonesia to South America. In turn, these altered atmospheric conditions can change strength and location of some of the jet streams. The bottom line is that during La Niña years winters are warmer than normal in the Southeast and cooler in the Northwest.

RECORD TEMPERATURES

According to the National Climate Extremes Committee, which is part of NOAA, the highest temperature ever recorded in the United States was 134°F at Greenland Ranch, California, on July 10, 1913. The record low of minus 80°F was recorded at Prospect Creek, Alaska, on January 23, 1971. The greatest 24-hour temperature change—103 degrees—occurred at Loma, Montana, between January 14 and 15, 1972.

 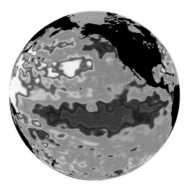

El Niño Year – November 1997   **La Niña Year – February 1999**

In an El Niño year (top left), warm waters, shown in red and white, build up on the coast of South America; cold waters build up in La Niña years (top right). Angry waves pound the California coast during a strong El Niño year (above).

CLOUDS, FOG, AND DEW

"I wield the flail of the lashing hail,
And whiten the green plains under,
And then again I dissolve it in rain
And laugh as I pass in thunder."

"THE CLOUD," PERCY BYSSHE SHELLEY

They are castles in the air, tufts of angel hair or puffs of sunset-pink cotton candy. They can be white stripes on a blue field, or dark gray eminences hovering menacingly over mountains. They are whirligigs reaching toward heaven, or purple funnels spiraling toward Earth.

Artists and poets have defined clouds in thousands of ways. But what—meteorologically speaking—are clouds? And what role do they play in weather?

Clouds typically cover almost two-thirds of the Earth, and they play a vital, if transitory, role in a key weather and climate process: the water cycle. Much of Earth's atmosphere consists of water vapor, an invisible gas. When warm air rises, it cools, and the water vapor in the parcel of air condenses and forms tiny water droplets or ice crystals. The droplets or crystals adhere to dust particles, making them visible, and vertical currents of air waft them skyward—as clouds. Clouds return the water to the earth and the oceans as rain.

Drifting in from the Pacific, advection fog fills undulating valleys of coastal redwoods and Sitka spruce on the northern California coast.

Clouds can also form when air hits against a mountain and is forced over the obstacle, cooling as it rises. If the air cools to its saturation point—the dew point—the water vapor condenses and becomes a cloud.

THE FATHER OF CLOUDS

Before 1800, no one really knew what clouds were. They were referred to poetically, or as vague essences floating in the sky. A young amateur scientist named Luke Howard helped change that. As a teenager, Howard got hooked on the atmosphere when volcanic dust from eruptions in Iceland settled over England, causing brilliant sunrises and sunsets. From then on, he kept a sketchbook of clouds. He never studied meteorology but became a pharmacist. Howard joined a group of "natural philosophers" who met to discuss papers they wrote on various scientific subjects. During the winter of 1802-1803, Howard read a paper he had written on classifications of clouds. His paper, which was very well received in the scientific community, forms the basis of the classification scheme we use today.

Howard divided clouds into basic shapes.

Cumulus (Latin for "heap"): Heaps of separated cloud masses with flat bottoms and cauliflower tops. These lumpy towers of clouds are usually found at low levels, below 6,500 feet. They are formed by updrafts of air, or thermals.

Stratus (Latin for "layer"): Layers or banks of clouds wider than they are thick. They are formed by widespread uplifts of air and tend to be gray and cover most of the sky. They are often accompanied by mist and drizzle.

Cirrus (Latin for "curl"): Wispy curls, like locks of hair. These are found high up in the atmosphere where water vapor is less abundant. Cirrus clouds consist mainly of ice crystals. Cirrus clouds are shaped by high-level winds.

Nimbus (Latin for "rain"): Clouds that generate precipitation. Nimbus clouds are generally low clouds, less than a mile high. CONTINUED ON PAGE 64

In nature's recycling program, the sun warms the Earth, and water vapor rises from lakes, rivers, oceans, plants, and soil—a process called evaporation. The oceans contribute 80 percent of this evaporation. Winds carry this water vapor around the globe, producing humidity. As the moisture climbs high into the atmosphere, it cools and loses its ability to contain water vapor. The excess water vapor condenses, forming tiny water droplets or ice crystals that adhere to dust particles and become visible as clouds. The clouds are held up by vertical currents of air, until the droplets or crystals inside become too heavy and fall back to Earth as rain, snow, hail, or sleet. The precipitation fills lakes, refreshes wetlands, flows into rivers and oceans, and filters through the ground to replenish aquifers. Some groundwater seeps back into rivers, streams, and oceans, and some evaporates back into the atmosphere from plants—a process known as transpiration. And the cycle begins again.

ON THE FOLLOWING PAGES: **Clouds, classified by appearance, take many shapes. Clockwise from top left: cirrus, nimbus, stratus, and cumulus. Each cloud type is formed under different conditions.**

ON PAGES 62-63: **A sunset-tinged lenticular cloud hugs the lee side of Colorado's Front Range. Lenticular clouds form when a large obstacle, such as the Front Range, blocks a strong air current.**

These four cloud types also come in variations and combinations, such as stratocumulus
(low, lumpy cloud layers with patches of blue
sky between the cloud elements); cirrostratus
(high, thin clouds that blanket the sky in ill-
defined sheets); cirrocumulus (high level
cumulus clouds combined with cirrus clouds,
indicating unstable air); nimbostratus (low,
dark, thick clouds of undefined shape, usually
indicating heavy precipitation); cumulonimbus
(tall clouds with anvil-shaped tops that can her-
ald storms); altocumulus, or wool-pack clouds
(patches or rolls of cloud joined together in a
sort of sheet); altostratus (pale, watery clouds
that form a translucent veil over the sun).

All together, there are almost a hundred
variations of clouds.

Some of the most beautiful clouds are
only visible between sunset and sunrise, and
only in the higher latitudes. These are the
very thin nacreous, mother-of-pearl-like
clouds found 12 to 18 miles above the Earth
and the even higher noctilucent, or night-
luminous, clouds.

While most clouds dwell in the first six
miles above the ground, noctilucent clouds
form about 50 miles up, near the top of the
mesosphere, where temperatures plunge to a
frigid minus 130°F. Composed of ice crystals,
bright, silvery noctilucent clouds are visible at
night because their height above Earth allows
them to escape the planet's shadow.

CONTRAILS

One type of cloud didn't exist in Luke
Howard's time: the contrails, or "condensation
trails," formed from the vapor spewed into the
atmosphere from jet planes flying at high alti-
tudes. The cold temperatures in the upper

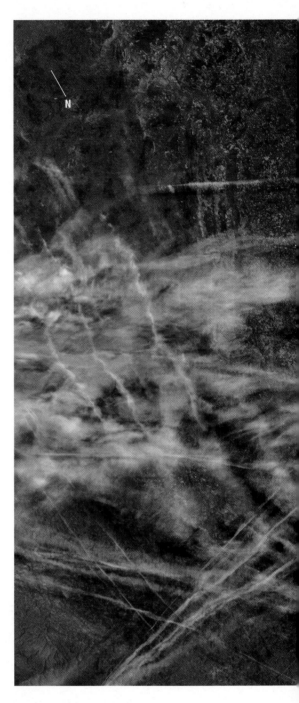

atmosphere turn the vapor into ice crystals that look like cirrus clouds.

Some scientists believe that these contrails may contribute to global warming. Writing
in the *Journal of Climate* in April 2004, researchers from the National Aeronautics and
Space Administration (NASA) reported that the cirrus clouds formed by contrails from

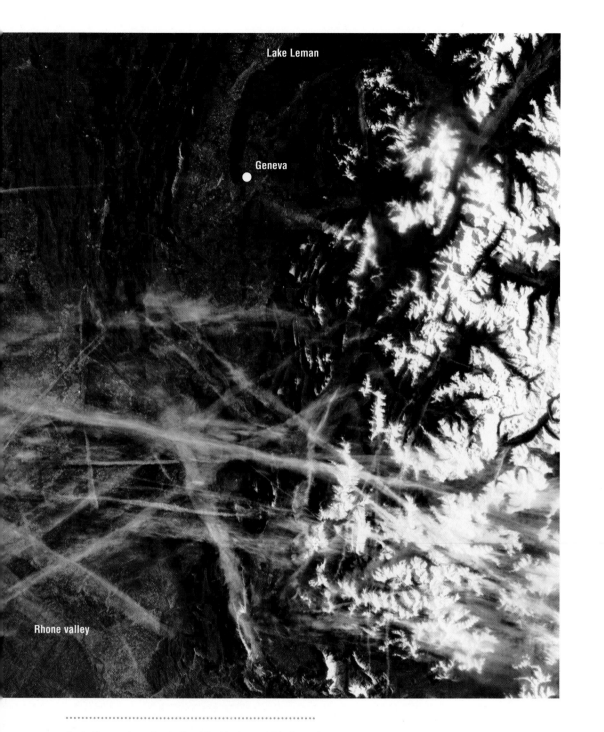

Lake Leman

Geneva

Rhone valley

Contrails, condensation trails etched by ice crystals formed
by the exhaust of jet planes, crisscross the sky over the
Rhone Valley in France and Switzerland. Scientists have
found that contrails can increase surface temperatures.

aircraft engine exhaust are capable of increasing temperatures enough to account for the warming trend that occurred in the United States between 1975 and 1994.

"This study indicates that contrails already have substantial regional effects where air traffic is heavy, such as over the United States," said Patrick Minnis, senior research scientist at NASA's Langley Research Center in Hampton, Virginia. "As air travel continues growing in other areas, the impact could become globally significant."

Cloud experts had a unique opportunity to assess the effects of contrails in the wake of the September 11, 2001, terrorist attacks, when flights over U.S. airspace were suspended. The scientists compared satellite imagery from September 11 to 13 with 30 years of cloud cover data, and correlated this information with temperature readings. They found that, under the clear skies that followed the September 11 attacks, the difference between daytime and nighttime temperatures grew between three and five degrees Fahrenheit. Contrails, they concluded, are narrowing the range of temperature between day and night, making days cooler by increasing the cloud cover and making nights warmer by providing an insulating blanket over the Earth.

CLOUDS, PRECIPITATION, AND CLIMATE

Clouds are harbingers of weather to come. Scattered cumulus clouds against a blue sky promise a fair, dry day. Massive gray thunderheads portend high winds and rain. High wispy curls mean a change in the weather.

Clouds don't necessarily mean rain. The water vapor droplets that make up clouds are usually too small and light to fall. But sometimes the droplets grow heavier by colliding and combining within a cloud. Or, ice crystals, which are heavier than water vapor, can form at the top of a cloud. When the ice crystals fall through the cloud, they pick up more water. In either case, when the ice crystals or droplets become too heavy for the cloud to hold them suspended in air, they fall—as rain, sleet, snow, or hail.

In addition to acting as watering cans, clouds modify the distribution of solar heat. They cool Earth by reflecting incoming sunlight back into the atmosphere. They help keep Earth warmer by trapping heat lost from Earth's surface and radiating it back to Earth.

Scientists are not sure which influence is stronger, and what the net effect of clouds on Earth's temperature is. But they are working to find out. Scientists from NASA, NOAA, and several universities are studying clouds, using satellites, airplanes, and computer models. When they finish, they hope to have answers to some important questions: Can clouds mitigate the effects of global warming? Or will global warming change clouds in a way that actually intensifies the problem?

A CLOUD ON THE GROUND

When a cloud hugs the ground, we call it fog. Or, as the American Meteorological Society's *Glossary of Weather and Climate* defines it, fog is "a visible aggregate of minute water droplets suspended in the atmosphere near the Earth's surface."

Rolling in atop Pacific waves, a thick fog blankets northern California. Fog can close airports and strand ships, but it can also inspire artists with its ethereal beauty and help quench the thirst of trees, plants, and animals.

Just as clouds come in many different varieties, so, too, does fog. Radiation fog or ground fog, the most common type of fog, occurs when the ground cools and causes condensation in the layers of air nearest the earth. It forms at night and usually dissipates early in the day, as soon as the sun has had a chance to warm the ground. Radiation fog drapes a veil of mysterious beauty over the land, and is never more beautiful that in its death throes, when the sun shines through and chases it away.

Advection fog is caused by the horizontal movement of mild, humid air over a cold surface. The fog that hovers over the ocean and other bodies of water is advection fog, as is fog that drifts down from the hillsides and fills the surrounding valleys.

Upslope fog occurs when winds blow moist air upward over higher terrain. As the air rises, it cools to below the dew point, and its water droplets condense.

SMOKE + FOG = SMOG

Fog can be both picturesque and deadly. It can close airports, cause automobile accidents, strand hikers. When mixed with pollutants in the air, fog becomes smog and threatens health and safety in other ways.

The term "smog" was coined by a British forecaster in 1905, who used it to describe the fog intensified by smoke

The smog that wrapped greater London in a noxious cocoon in December 1952 blocked out the sun and snarled traffic (left). Londoners donned masks to keep the sooty mix out of their lungs (above).

that often hung over Great Britain's urban centers, where most homes were heated by coal fires and where factories belched black smoke. One of the worst occurrences of this phenomenon—the Great Smog of 1952—descended on London on December 5 and wrapped the city and surrounding areas in a noxious cocoon for five days.

It was a cold December, and people had been burning more coal. On the night of December 4, there were clear skies and a blanket of moist air near the ground. A light wind stirred the moist air—mixed with the smoke of thousands of chimneys—upward. As the smoke-laden air rose, it cooled and condensed, turning into a thick, sooty fog 325 to 650 feet deep. A high pressure area in the atmosphere created an inversion layer, preventing the condensation and polluted air from dissipating. Each day for five days, the fog thickened. Londoners couldn't see the sun—some couldn't even see their feet.

Cattle grazing in nearby Smithfield were asphyxiated. Trains virtually stopped running. A performance of the Sadler Wells ballet was interrupted when the air in the theatre became

DEW AND FROST

Dew strings a pearl necklace of glistening water droplets across a morning lawn, then disappears as the sun climbs higher in the sky.

On colder mornings, frost leaves a crusty white layer on gardens and windowpanes.

Dew and frost occur when night cools the ground and the air just above it to the dew point temperature—the temperature at which the water vapor in a given parcel of air condenses. When water vapor condenses, it has to alight on something, so it forms on grass, flowers, plants, and other objects on or near the ground. If the temperature of the ground, or the objects just above it, is above freezing, dew forms. If the temperature is below freezing, the water vapor turns directly into frost.

Sun-sparkled dew strings festive lights on a spider's web. Cooler nighttime temperatures turn water vapor in the air into tiny water droplets that alight on plants, grass, or anything on or near the ground.

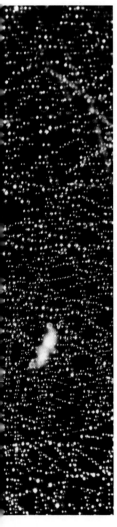

too noxious for both performers and onlookers. And at least 4,000 people—possibly as many as 12,000—died of respiratory problems exacerbated by the smog. Deaths from bronchitis and pneumonia increased sevenfold. Undertakers ran out of coffins, and florists worked overtime on funeral wreaths.

Despite the disruptions and deaths that it caused, the Great Smog of 1952 did some good: It spurred legislation that mandated reduced emissions and cleaner fuels. Slum clearance and the spread of central heating have also abated the pollution that long created smog in England.

But the danger from smog persists. In the Los Angeles, California, area, for example, exhaust fumes from automobiles mix with cool, moist air from the Pacific to form smog. The mountains behind the city form a basin. And an inversion layer of warm air caused by a high pressure cell typically hangs over the area. The mountains and the inversion layer combine to trap the smog so that it lingers for long periods.

DEFENSES AGAINST FOG

Reducing emissions—from automobiles and industries and power plants—can cut smog. But fog, a natural phenomenon, will always be with us. Better forecasting can mitigate the accidents caused by fog, and so can some technologies, such as navigation aids for ships and airplanes. One of the oldest technological defenses against fog is the lighthouse.

Since the first lighthouse appeared in the harbor of Alexandria, Egypt, in the third century B.C., these beacons have guided travelers to safety with light. But since fog can obliterate light, keepers often had to use sound to warn sailors of danger. Canons, Chinese gongs, bells, reed horns, and sirens were some of the devices they employed. Today, deep, guttural foghorns sound the alarm. Point Bonita Lighthouse, at the south entrance to San Francisco Bay, which Sir Francis Drake missed because it was shrouded in fog, sends out two sound blasts every 30 seconds in dense fog, which actually intensifies the sound.

THE PLUS SIDE OF FOG

Not everyone considers fog a menace. Many artists have exulted in it. English artist J. M. W. Turner reportedly used to fling open his shutters during London "pea soupers" and cry "What dazzlement!" And French painter Claude Monet used the fog to add mysterious beauty to his Impressionist canvases.

In some rain-poor parts of the world, people are actually harvesting fog. For example, the people of Chungungo, Chile, on the edge of the vast Atacama Desert, are harvesting the *camanchacas,* the frequent coastal fogs driven inland by the wind, for drinking water. Before the project, initially funded by the Canadian government, got underway, water had to be trucked into Chungungo. The village population was shrinking, as young people left for wetter ground. Today, there are four hectares of community vegetable

ON THE FOLLOWING PAGES: **Smokestacks shrouded in morning fog belch pollutants from pulp mills into the air on the northern California coast. Under certain atmospheric conditions, smoke, added to fog, can create noxious smog.**

gardens, trees planted along the road, and a municipal park. People are installing showers in their homes, and clothes can be washed more frequently. The village is largely self-sufficient as far as water is concerned, and the population is growing.

Fifty collectors, consisting of nylon net strung between wooden poles, face into the wind. As the fog hits the net, the water vapor in the fog condenses into droplets and falls into a collecting tank. Experts estimate that about 30 percent of the water in fog can be harvested.

Other fog collecting projects are underway in other parts of Chile and in other countries, including Peru, Ecuador, Mexico, and Namibia.

COLOR THE SKY BLUE

Sunlight is composed of a spectrum of colors: red, orange, yellow, green, blue, and violet. The violet and blue colors at one end of the spectrum have shorter wavelengths than the reds and oranges at the other end. Gas molecules in the atmosphere scatter the violet and blue end of the spectrum more effectively than the other colors, so the light scattered down to Earth appears predominantly blue. (Human eyes are more sensitive to blue light than to violet, or else the sky would appear violet rather than blue.) This principle is known as the Rayleigh scattering, after an English physicist.

RED SKY AT NIGHT

At sunrise or sunset, when the sun lies low on the horizon, the sun's light must pass through a greater thickness of gas molecules. During this longer journey, much of the violet and blue light is scattered along the way and the light that reaches our eyes late in the day or at dawn appears red or orange.

In the Northern Hemisphere's temperate zones, weather systems often come from the west. High pressure systems mean clear skies in the west, and the reddest sunsets. The sinking air of a high pressure system keeps the dust and pollution low. The gas molecules scatter the shorter wavelengths of light—the violets and blues—and leave the longer wavelengths, oranges and reds. Since high pressure systems usually bring good weather, the next day is likely to be fair. But if the eastern sky looks red in the morning, the high pressure system has already passed through and will most likely be replaced by a low pressure system. This is the basis for a weather proverb that actually originated in the Gospel of Matthew: "Red sky at night, sailors' delight; red sky in the morning, sailors' warning."

DECONSTRUCTING RAINBOWS

When the sun is shining but the atmosphere contains raindrops, multicolored stripes of color—rainbows—decorate the portion of the sky opposite the sun. When we see a rainbow,

As the sun sinks lower on the horizon, its light takes longer to reach the human eye. Much of the blue in the spectrum is lost along the way, letting the red shine through, as here in Arizona.

ON THE FOLLOWING PAGES: **Rainbows, such as this** one over the Grand Canyon, form when the sun shines through raindrops in the atmosphere. The sunlight is fractured through the prism of a raindrop.

we are really looking at all the colors contained in sunlight through the prism of a raindrop. Sunlight contains all the colors of the spectrum, from violet to red. When the colors are combined, sunlight looks white to the eye. When sunlight beams into a drop of water, it is refracted, or bent, because water has a different density than air. When bent, the beam of sunlight separates into its component colors. The light reflects from the drop's inner surface, then refracts out of the drop, and is bent again, with some colors of the spectrum bent at greater angles than others. That's why rainbows look like arcs. In fact, they're circles. If the Earth were not in our line of vision, we would see full circles of color. When the sun is low on the horizon—or when you are very high, as in an airplane—you can see more of the circle.

Sometimes, you can see a fainter second rainbow outside the first arc. Double rainbows occur when raindrops high in the atmosphere reflect the sun's light twice before the ray reemerges from the drop. This produces a sort of mirror image, where the color sequence is reversed, with red on the inside of the curve rather than the outside.

Lunar rainbows, or moonbows, are seen much less often than the daylight variety. Moonlight is really reflected sunlight, with the same color makeup. When moonlight hits drops of rain, the raindrop acts as a prism and separates the light into the colors of the spectrum. Because of the lower light at night, however, we usually see the colors as a ghostly white bow. Moonbows are best seen when the moon is full and in a pollution-free place without much artificial light, such as on the sea.

FLASHES OF GREEN

"I looked for it for about 40 years before I finally saw it," said Jim Taylor, a charter boat captain who takes guests for cruises around the British Virgin Islands on his sailing yacht *Andiamo*. "I first heard about it when I was in the Navy, in Vietnam. I was on an LST

An emerald green flash slices the horizon off California's coast. This flash is produced when the dense atmosphere at sunset bends the sun's light into colored arcs. The blue color is scattered, leaving a fleeting flash of bright green.

[landing ship tank] that picked cargo up in Vung Tao and Saigon and took it to bases in the Mekong Delta. A couple of times, we sailed to the Philippines and Taiwan, through the South China Sea, and, at sunset, we'd all stand on deck and look for the green flash. But we never saw it, and I wasn't sure it was real. After that, I always looked for it on vacations in the Bahamas and the Caribbean, but still never saw it. Then, last year, we were on a charter cruise and anchored off Anagada, in the British Virgins. You anchor into the wind, so you're facing east, and the sun is off the stern. We were watching the sun set. You need an unobstructed view of the horizon, and, ideally, it should be cloud-free. That evening, there were clouds just above the horizon, but there was a small gap between the clouds and the sea. Just as the sun sank, a bright, very distinct green flash appeared in the gap under the clouds."

Captain Taylor is following in the wake of a long line of mariners who counted themselves lucky to see this atmospheric color show. The search for the flash took on an almost mythical aura after 1882 with the publication of Jules Verne's novel, *Le Rayon Vert,* or *The Green Ray.* Verne described the phenomenon as "a green which no artist could ever obtain on his palette, a green of which neither the varied tints of vegetation nor the shades of the most limpid sea could ever produce the like! If there is a green in Paradise, it cannot be but of this shade, which most surely is the true green of Hope."

WHAT EXACTLY IS THE GREEN FLASH?

First, let's talk about what it isn't. It's not the green afterimage in your retina after you've looked directly into the setting sun, although many people confuse the two.

The true green flash is a fleeting slice of bright green light on the horizon the instant after sunset—or just before sunrise. It is produced by the force that gives us rainbows—

the dispersion of sunlight into different colors when it enters particular atmospheric phenomena. At sunset, the denser atmosphere near the Earth's surface acts as a prism, bending the sun's rays and dispersing colored arcs just above and below the sun's orange orb. Light at the blue end of the spectrum bends most; light at the red end of the spectrum bends least. What we see at sunset is a vertical stack of sun images, with the blue image on top, the red at the bottom and the green in between. Due to the Rayleigh scattering, the blue light is dispersed widely across the sky, so the light we see has much of the blue removed from it. Partly due to this scattering and party due to the physiological properties of the human eye, we see the flash as blue-green, or emerald.

Caution: Never look directly into the sun, even when it's setting. You could suffer permanent vision damage.

Rings or haloes around the sun or moon were once considered harbingers of doom. Today, scientists know that light shining through thin cirrus or cirrostratus clouds creates this optical phenomenon. The clouds are packed with ice crystals, which refract, or bend, the rays of light around the sun or moon.

Sun dogs, so called because they stick close to their master, are bright spots to either side of the sun, just outside the halo. Sometimes called "mock suns," they are caused by sunlight passing through ice crystals inside clouds.

Although haloes and sun dogs don't necessarily portend disaster, they do indicate that bad weather may be on the way, since the moist rising air that forms ice crystals is associated with low pressure systems.

The Specter of the Brocken may sound like a novel by Sherlock Holmes or an opera by Richard Wagner but it's really the historical name associated with an optical phenomenon commonly known as a "glory." The Brocken, a high peak in the Harz Mountains of central Germany, lies above cloud level, and its lower slopes are typically shrouded in fog. Climbers emerging above the fog sometimes saw mysterious giant shadows with colored rings around their heads. The figures were actually the climbers' own shadows cast over the fog, and the rings of color were produced by the water droplets in the clouds and fog, which break up the sun's light and bend it around the shadow. Today, glories are often seen ringing the shadow of an airplane on the clouds.

MIRAGES

Most everyone has experienced the desert, or inferior, mirage. You see what looks like a pool of water on the highway or desert ahead. As you approach, the tantalizing image—an optical illusion—disappears.

In a desert mirage, hot, light air near the ground bends light rays upward toward the colder, denser air above it. The "pool of water" we thought we saw was actually the image of the blue sky refracted by the hot air near the ground. The illusionary image is called an "inferior" mirage because the something seen is below its actual location.

An Arctic, or superior, mirage, occurs under the opposite atmospheric conditions—when the air near the surface is much colder than the air above it. Under these conditions, light rays are bent downward. As a result, we see objects as closer and taller than they really are. This phenomenon makes it possible for people to see objects beyond the normal

Sun dogs illumine a landscape of ice and snow near Churchill, Manitoba. Hexagonal ice crystals in cirrostratus clouds bend the sun's light to create these mock suns, which appear most often when the sun lies low in the sky.

horizon. Some historians believe that the Vikings used Arctic mirages as a navigational aid in early voyages to Greenland and North America.

Another complex type of mirage is the Fata Morgana, named for Morgan le Fay, the sorceress in the King Arthur legends. The enchantress lived in an ornate undersea castle, which she sometimes made appear on the horizon, luring sailors to their deaths; the Fata Morgana mirage appears as a ghostly castle rising out of the sea. The mirage occurs when there are alternating layers of warm and cold air above the surface. Instead of traveling straight through these layers, the light bends in a complex path, transforming objects on the horizon, such as islands, cliffs, and icebergs, into fairyland castles.

The northern lights, or aurora borealis, stage nature's most spectacular light show in latitudes above 60º north, sending diaphanous curtains tinted yellow, green, violet, and red dancing across the sky.

English sea captains first reported the phenomenon in the Strait of Messina, between Italy and Sicily, in 1818. It is also seen in high mountain valleys and in Arctic seas. Reports of these mirages inspired a poem, "Fata Morgana" by Henry Wadsworth Longfellow, which ends:

And forever before me gleams
The shining city of song
In the beautiful land of dreams.

But when I would enter the gate
Of that golden atmosphere
It is gone, and I wander and wait
For the vision to reappear.

THE NORTHERN LIGHTS

The northern lights, or aurora borealis—and their southern cousins, the aurora australis— are nature's most lavish light show. Diaphanous curtains of light swirl through the night sky, changing colors and shapes and creating a phosphorescent glow.

What exactly are the northern lights?

The Inuit people thought they were torches used by those already in heaven to guide new arrivals. In medieval Europe, they were thought to be the ghosts of dead knights continuing their battles in the after-life. In fact, they are creatures of the sun.

The sun emits highly charged particles of energy that travel into space at speeds of more than 200 miles a second. The particles form a cloud, or plasma, called the solar wind. When the plasma meets Earth's magnetic field, some of the particles are trapped and follow lines of magnetic force down into the ionosphere, the upper part of Earth's atmosphere. The particles collide with gases in the ionosphere and glow in shades of red, green, blue, and violet, depending on which of the gases they collide with. Oxygen creates red or green light, depending on altitude, while nitrogen colors the sky blue or violet. Because of the interaction between the solar wind and Earth's magnetic field, the northern lights move constantly, like giant curtains weaving across the night sky.

PRECIPITATION:
RAIN, SNOW, FLOODS, AND DROUGHT

"Let it come down."

MACBETH, ACT III, SCENE 3, WILLIAM SHAKESPEARE

When clouds become too heavily laden with tiny water droplets, gravity overcomes air resistance and pulls the droplets to Earth in the form of rain. Turbulence within a cloud causes the droplets to hit other droplets and merge with them, and the heavy droplets fall to earth. Often, this turbulence results from frontal activity, when a warm and a cold front meet.

Snow begins to form when the water vapor in the atmosphere that condenses on small dust particles freezes. The ice crystals grow and merge with other ice crystals to form snowflakes. When the snowflakes gain enough mass, they fall to the ground as snow.

When ice crystals melt partially on their way to Earth and then refreeze as they meet colder air near the surface, raindrop-size pieces of sleet fall to the ground. If the layer of cold air near the ground isn't thick enough, the raindrops fall as freezing rain. When they hit the cold ground, they glaze it with ice.

Rain fills reservoirs and supplies drinking water. It makes grass and crops grow. It nourishes and cools the Earth. And snow paints winter wonderlands, delighting children and skiers.

Spattered on glass, raindrops paint an impressionist picture of trees outside a window. Too much rain can swell rivers and inundate land with destructive floods; too little can choke the land with dust.

But precipitation—or the lack of it—can also cause floods, droughts, and blizzards, bringing disruption, destruction, and death. Let's look at what happens when too much rain, or too little, falls to Earth and at how much damage millions of tiny snowflakes can do.

DELUGES, DESTRUCTION

In China, floods have wreaked havoc since ancient times, testing the mettle of emperors, who have based their legitimacy on their ability to control flooding. The most devastating and frequent floods have occurred along the Yangtze, the longest river in Asia and the third longest in the world, after the Nile and the Amazon. In the past 2,000 years, the Yangtze has flooded more than a thousand times.

Born in the mountains of Tibet, the river descends to the Yunnan Plateau, spills into the Sichuan Basin, enters the scenic Three Gorges, and swirls through the fertile plains of China's heartland. Some 700 major tributaries feed its waters. When rains swell the river, there is not enough channel capacity to hold the water. It overflows its banks, inundating the plains where one-third of the population lives and some 40 percent of the country's grain and more than 30 percent of the cotton grows. An ancient system of levees is the sole protection against inundation, but all too often, the levees leak and fail.

In the summer of 1931, after a two-year drought, stationary storm centers lingered over the headwaters of the Lishua and Yuangshi Rivers, which feed the Yangtze. The powerful, rain-swollen rivers broke the Yangtze's main dike in 300 places, submerging an area the size of Belgium. By the time the waters receded a hundred days later, 3.7 million people were dead from drowning, disease, or starvation. Some 3.3 million hectares of farmland were ruined, and 1.8 million houses had collapsed.

Since that time, China has initiated measures that have, at least, mitigated flood damages, and officials are placing high hopes on the Three Gorges Dam, scheduled for completion in 2009.

But even state-of-the-art engineering cannot prevent the devastation of floods. Witness the Great Midwest Flood of 1993, one of the most damaging natural disasters ever to hit the United States. The toll: $15 billion in

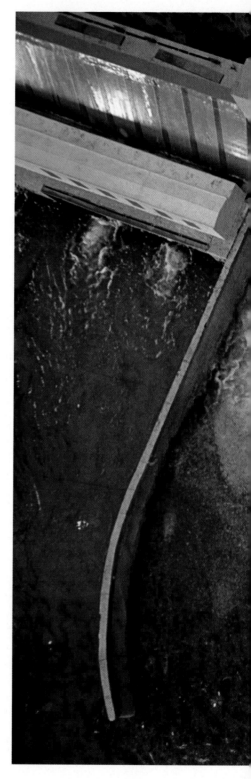

長江三峡水利枢纽模

Stemming the Yangtze's flow, a worker operates a sluice gate designed to tame China's Yangtze River, which has brought devastating floods more than a thousand times in the past 2,000 years.

ON THE FOLLOWING PAGES: Shimmering in the sunset, China's Yangtze River carves its way through a plain that will soon be inundated by the Three Gorges Dam. The dam is scheduled for completion in 2009.

property damage, 50 deaths, and thousands of people evacuated, some for months and some never to return to their homes. More than 10,000 homes were destroyed, and 75 towns were completly submerged. At least 15 million acres of farmland were inundated. Barge traffic on the Mississippi and Missouri Rivers stopped dead for almost two months. Bridges, interstate highways, and railroad traffic were affected, and ten commercial airports were flooded.

WHAT TRIGGERED THE 1993 FLOOD?

The flood was set in motion the winter before, with heavy snowfalls whose melt filled the rivers to the brim. Then, in the spring of 1993, a strong high pressure system moved over the Southeast and stalled there. While the South and mid-Atlantic enjoyed fair sunny weather, winds around the high pressure area pushed moisture-laden air from the Gulf of Mexico into the upper Midwest. The warm, moist air collided with cool, dry Canadian air that rode in with the jet stream. The clash of these two air masses resulted in heavy rains, which could not be blown eastward by the prevailing winds because the high pressure area blocked the way. The rainfall continued from April through August—bringing more than three feet of rain in parts of Iowa, Kansas, and Missouri, saturating the soil and causing more than a hundred rivers to overflow. And the rain fell steadily, almost daily, most of the summer.

By early June, the midwestern soil was saturated to capacity, and streams were full. As the rains continued, there was nowhere for the water to go other than into the river channels. The Missouri River crested at a record 48.9 feet at Kansas City on July 27, while the Mississippi crested at a record 49.5 feet at St. Louis on August 1. Some 92 places along the Mississippi saw new record crests during the summer of 1993.

FLASH FLOODING

Flash floods—the deadliest and most fast-moving type of flooding—occur within six hours of a rainstorm, after a dam or levee failure, or with the sudden release of water by an ice jam. People are often caught off guard by these floods, which can turn placid streams into raging rivers in minutes. Flash floods rip out trees, topple buildings, and sometimes trigger damaging mudslides.

On June 9, 1972, Rapid City, South Dakota, experienced 15 inches of rain in five hours. The resultant flood took 238 lives and caused $164 million in damages, according to the National Weather Service. Five years later, on April 18, 1997, the Red River poured over dikes in Grand Forks, North Dakota, flooding large areas of the town and forcing nearly 50,000 people out of their homes.

Like the Yangtze, the Mississippi has a long, recurring history of flooding. After record flooding in 1927, the U.S. Army Corps of Engineers went to work to tame the river, building a system of levees that minimized flood damage and improved navigation. But the public confidence inspired by this feat may have backfired. People moved into the floodplain, turning wetlands into farmland and towns. Without wetlands to soak up the excess water, the 1993 flood devastated farms, villages, even cities.

When the Red River inundated Grand Forks, North Dakota, in 1997, fire broke out in several downtown buildings. Fire engines ploughed valiantly through flooded streets, but water pressure was low and hydrants hard to find.

Runoff from melting snow can also cause significant flooding. In January 1996, for example, snowmelt triggered major flooding in Virginia, New York, Vermont, and on the upper reaches of the Ohio River. The floods caused $1.5 billion in damages and took 33 lives. The next year, snowmelt caused flooding along the Red River of the North (in North Dakota, Minnesota, and Manitoba, Canada), resulting in $4 billion worth of damages.

PREDICTING FLOODS

On average, 140 Americans die each year due to floods. The best weapon against floods is accurate and timely forecasting. Thousands of stream-gauging stations scattered around the United States constantly monitor the stage (the water depth above a "normal" level) and flow (the volume of water moving past a certain point in a certain period of time) in major

rivers and urban streams. This data is automatically relayed to the National Weather Service, which uses complex mathematical models of how individual rivers and streams respond to rainfall and snowmelt. In recent years, great strides have been made in assessing the danger posed by melting snow. Once, weather service employees simply measured the depth of snow. But different kinds of snow have varying levels of water content. Fluffy snow, for example, contains less water than heavy, slushy snow. Today, NOAA uses a plane, the Shrike Commander, to obtain highly accurate snow measurements. A sophisticated gamma radiation spectrometer aboard the aircraft measures the low levels of gamma radiation from trace elements in the upper layers of soil. Water mass in the snow blocks the signal—the deeper the snow the weaker the signal. Analysts use the difference between the radiation measurements made over bare ground and those made over snow-covered ground to calculate the amount of water in snow cover.

In the summer of 1993, despite valiant efforts to control it, the mighty Mississippi broke through and poured over countless levees erected to protect farmlands and towns from rising flood waters, resulting from incessant rains.

A dust storm rips through a Great Plains farm during
the Dust Bowl of the 1930s. By 1934, prolonged
drought had rendered an estimated 34 million acres
of land useless for farming.

DRY DEATH AND BLACK BLIZZARDS

Meteorologists also use a number of factors to predict the opposite of flooding: drought. Each Thursday, the National Weather Service, in partnership with several other agencies, puts out a Drought Monitor for the United States, based on a combination of drought indicators, including soil moisture estimates and stream flow data. But such sophisticated monitoring techniques did not exist in the 1930s, when farmers in the Great Plains suffered a prolonged drought of near-biblical proportions, an event now known as the infamous Dustbowl.

According to the American Meteorological Society, a drought is an extended interval of abnormally dry weather sufficiently prolonged for the lack of water to cause a serious hydrologic imbalance, resulting in crop damage, water supply shortage, and more. In the case of the Dustbowl, the drought lasted nearly a decade.

Severe drought hit the midwestern and southern plains in 1931. Crops died, and dust from overplowed, overgrazed land swirled through the skies in "black blizzards." The number of these dust storms steadily increased. In 1933, there were 38. The drought uprooted farm families from their homes, turning them into wandering paupers. As John Steinbeck wrote in *The Grapes of Wrath*, "Now the wind grew strong and hard and it worked at the rain crust in the corn fields. Little by little the sky was darkened by the mixing dust, and the wind felt over the earth, loosened the dust, and carried it away. The wind grew stronger. The rain crust broke and the dust lifted up out of the fields and drove gray plumes into the air like sluggish smoke. The corn threshed the wind and made a dry, rushing sound. The finest dust did not settle back to earth now, but disappeared into the darkening sky."

By the summer of 1934, the drought covered more than three-fourths of the nation, impacting 27 states severely. An estimated 34 million acres of cultivated land had been rendered useless for farming, and 100 million acres had lost all or most of their topsoil. In 1935, the Soil Conservation Service was established, paying farmers to practice soil-conserving agricultural techniques. By 1938, conservation measures had reduced the amount of blowing soil by 65 percent, but the drought continued. Not until the fall of 1939 did the rains come, ending the eight-and-a-half-year drought.

WHAT CAUSED THE DUSTBOWL?

Unwise agricultural practices exacerbated the situation, but, in a time of normal rainfall, nature would have tolerated the shortsighted farming and grazing methods. The rains simply never came. Normally, moist air from the Gulf of Mexico flows to the Midwest and waters CONTINUED ON PAGE 100

ON THE FOLLOWING PAGES: **Braving a Dust Bowl blizzard, an Oklahoma farmer and his sons trudge across parched earth no longer fit for farming. The Dust Bowl turned many farm families into wandering paupers.**

ON PAGES 98-99: **By the summer of 1934, drought covered more than three-fourths of the United States and was the leading news story for close to a decade.**

Dust Storms
aten to Turn
d Into Desert

CITY, March 26 (UP)
dust storm

DUST DAMAGE
SENDS
MERS FIGHTT
TOP LOSSES R
UST STOR

BLA K GALE
AGAIN HOWLS
IN SOUTHWEST

FLYI
BLIZ

Flying
is

Storm Brings
fering to Hard-
Section

an and Beast Forced
Refuge in Buil

Black B
of New

Swe

IN TWO WEEKS, OR CROP
DUST BOWL WILL BE TOTAL
LOSS, FARM EXPERTS ASSERT

This spri
evere

ansas,
and N

LEGISLATION
NECESSARY
FIGHTING

ST STORMS RAGE
OM KANSAS WEST
AR AS CALIFORNIA

Two
As

Two ai
land at an
miles south
port Tuesda
were caug
storm that
at the airpo
One of

t of Year in 'Nation's Bread Basket
rch Services Halted; Second in Two
ys Blackens Skies at Guymon, Okla.

...NG THRU DUST BOWL WORSE THA...
...ZARDS, SAYS HERNDON, FAMO...

His reas...

...zzard
...Mexico
...ping East

...Mahoma Panhandle
...thwest Tip of
...as Are Hit

THREE YEAR OLD BENS...
SURVIVES ALMOST 20...
RAGING DUST STOR...

...LAD WALKS INTO FARM EIG...
FROM HIS HOME WHILE 500...
ERS HUNT IN VAIN

...ittle three year old boy of Two...
...other's arms today, after he had...
...night and Monday morning.
...dust storm of Sunday afte...
...ittle Ewell Steven Benson Jr.," walke...
...ree and a half miles south of Two Butte...
Monday morning after he had been...
...o'clock Sunday afternoon...
...UST home.
...home.

PRAIRA...
PRAY

Dust-Bow...
Plea W...
Yea...

...Planes Make Forced Landings
...ack Blizzard Hides Airport

...nes were forced to
...mergency field eight
...f the municipal air-
...afternoon when they
...in a sudden dust
...uced the visibil...

The...
Serv...
Holl...
from...
make...

Dust Storm Halts
Colora...

VICTIM
STOR...

the plains with rain. But a large high pressure system became lodged in the upper atmosphere above the center of the country, blocking the moist air from the Gulf.

New research by scientists at the National Aeronautics and Space Administration (NASA) has recently fingered an unlikely culprit: ocean temperatures. Using a computer model developed with satellite data, the scientists found that cooler-than-average tropical Pacific Ocean temperatures combined with warmer-than-normal tropical Atlantic Ocean temperatures created the atmospheric conditions that turned the country's breadbasket into a disaster area. The sea surface temperature anomalies contributed to a weakened low-level jet stream and changed the course of the jet stream. Normally, this ribbon of fast-moving air flows westward over the Gulf of Mexico and then heads north, dumping rain over the Great Plains. But the weakened jet stream traveled farther south instead.

"Just beginning to understand what occurred is really critical to understanding future droughts and the links to global climate change issues we're experiencing today," said Siegfried Schubert of NASA's Goddard Space Flight Center, the principal author of the study, which was published in the journal *Science*.

DROUGHT IN THE SAHEL

In the drought that gripped Africa's Sahel, a broad band at the southern edge of the Sahara, from 1970 through the mid-1980s, the blizzards were not black but red, as red dust that used to be soil blew across the parched area, sometimes reaching as far as Miami, Florida. Crops withered, animals wasted away, starvation was widespread, and vultures stalked the parched land. The drought in the Sahel claimed more than 600,000 lives over the course of 15 years. Although the Sahel drought was initially blamed on bad agricultural practices, a number of other possibilities have been raised.

According to a group of scientists in Australia and Canada, pollution from power plants in North America and Europe may have helped trigger the drought. Minute particles of sulfur dioxide may have altered the physics of cloud formation, reducing rainfall in Africa by as much as 50 percent, said the scientists.

"The Sahelian drought may be due to a combination of natural variability and atmospheric aerosols," said Leon Rotstayn, a principal author of the study, which was published in the *Journal of Climate* in August 2002.

Other studies point to ocean temperatures as a critical factor in Sahel droughts.

Using a computer model to simulate the rainfall in the Sahel from 1930 to 2000, the scientists found a strong correlation between warmer waters in the Indian Ocean near Africa and the lack of rainfall in the Sahel. The warmer-than-average waters weakened the monsoon, reducing rainfall. The model may be able to help predict future rainfall in the Sahel, alerting policy makers in time to make preparations. It may also have important implications for droughts in other places.

While it may be impossible to prevent droughts in this vulnerable region, scientists and government officials from the United States and all over the world are working together to

Periodic droughts plague the Sahel, a broad swath of land at the southern edge of the Sahara. The droughts decimate farmland and, in some places, allow the desert to encroach, as at the above farm in Mauritania.

avert future drought-caused famines in Africa. The Famine Early Warning Systems Network, funded by the U.S. Agency for International Development, monitors natural and man-made causes of drought and famine to provide time for policymakers to take preventive action.

FLOODS, DROUGHTS, AND EL NIÑO

The Peru Current, sometimes called the Humboldt Current, slices like a knife of icy water through the warmer seas of the Pacific off South America, and it teems with anchovies, prized by gourmets and a major ingredient in animal feed. But every two to seven years, around Christmas time, the cold waters are replaced by anchovy-killing warm waters, which Peruvian fishermen nicknamed El Niño, for the Christ Child who also comes at Christmas time.

El Niño does more than decimate the anchovy crop. It has important implications for weather events far from Peru. El Niño has been blamed for, among other things: increased rainfall in the southern United States, drought in the Western Pacific, brush-fires in Australia, water shortages in Bangkok, haze in Southeast Asia, whale beachings in the Falkland Islands, and famine in North Korea. How can a little cold water wreak so much havoc?

According to the National Oceanic and Atmospheric Administration (NOAA), El Niño is real, but exactly why it occurs is still theory. Scientists believe that El Niño events occur due to a complex interaction between the surface layers of the ocean and the overlying atmosphere in the tropical Pacific. This interaction seems to have a ripple effect on weather in far-flung areas of the globe. El Niño may have contributed to the 1993 flood on the Mississippi, and the 1995 California floods and to drought conditions in South America, Africa, and Australia.

The winter of 1997-98 saw one of the strongest El Niños on record.

El Niño has a female counterpart, La Niña, characterized by unusually cold ocean temperatures in the equatorial Pacific. La Niña often brings drier weather to most of the United States. The La Niña of the winter of 1998-99 may have been responsible for droughts and wildfires that plagued the southern states, from Virginia to Texas, in 1999.

"MIRACLES OF BEAUTY"

The ice crystals that make up snowflakes line up in specific ways determined by the molecular structure of water. The result is a lattice-like, symmetrical, six-sided shape. But, as they fall from the sky, the ice crystals meet very diverse atmospheric conditions, which help determine their individual

WHAT MAKES SNOW WHITE?

Snow is made up of individual, clear ice crystals. Each crystal is a tiny prism. When a beam of sunlight enters a bank of snow, the multitudinous ice crystals scatter the wavelengths of the spectrum quickly—giving no preference to any color of the spectrum. The human eye receives equal amounts of each color of the spectrum, and interprets this as white, the color of sunlight. When snow is tightly compressed, as in a glacier, light can penetrate much deeper into it. The longer the light beam's journey, the more wavelengths it loses from the red end of the spectrum. Since preference is given to the other end of the spectrum, the eye interprets icy snow as blue.

Pillows of fresh snow each hold millions of snowflakes a fraction of an inch wide. The snowflakes consist of even smaller crystals, whose shapes are determined by the atmospheric conditions they meet as they fall.

forms. In warmer air, for instance, the crystals can begin to melt. The partially melted ice acts like glue, bonding crystals into larger flakes. If the air the crystals encounter is very dry, they turn into prisms and columns. And at high humidity, crystals, depending on the temperature, take long, needle-like shapes or turn into fern-like dendrites. In 1951, an International Commission on Snow and Ice set up a classification system for snowflakes. According to this system, snowflakes come in seven principal types: plates, stellar crystals, columns, needles, spatial dendrites, capped columns, and irregular forms.

Scientists have studied snow crystals and snowflakes for hundreds of years. The first scientific reference that we know of was by astronomer Johannes Kepler, who published a 1611 treatise called *On the Six-Cornered Snowflake*, which raised questions that scientists couldn't yet answer. French philosopher and mathematician René Descartes also studied snow crystals, writing that "it is impossible for men to make anything so exact."

A snowflake's shape depends on how quickly it formed. In images by Wilson Bentley, the first snowflake photographer, the plain flake (top right) formed quickly, in cold air and low humidity; the fern-like crystal (top center) formed slowly, in warmer, humid air.

A self-educated Vermont farmer named Wilson Bentley, who lived from 1865 to 1931, adapted a microscope to a bellows camera. After years of trial and error, he became the first person to photograph a snow crystal, in 1885.

"Under the microscope, I found that snowflakes were miracles of beauty, and it seemed a shame that this beauty should not be seen and appreciated by others," Bentley wrote.

To make sure this beauty wouldn't be lost, Bentley meticulously photographed more than 5,000 snowflakes.

Although Bentley's photographs strengthened the popular belief that no two snowflakes are exactly alike, new evidence seems to disprove it. In 1988, scientist Nancy Knight of the National Center for Atmospheric Research, who was conducting a study on clouds, looked at snow crystals collected on a glass slide at the end of a rod extended from an aircraft flying between two layers of cirrus clouds over Wassau, Wisconsin. Dr. Knight found two that were identical under a microscope.

"To totally disprove this often quoted bit of folk wisdom that no two snowflakes are alike, you would have to look at their atomic structure, which is impossible to do because snow crystals melt," Dr. Knight, who is now semiretired, said in an interview. "But we did find two that were identical in appearance."

Scientists at Caltech are now disproving Descartes' statement that "it is impossible for men to make anything so exact." They're making snowflakes in the laboratory.

"While studying the physics of how snow crystals form and grow, I also became interested in the art of growing synthetic snowflakes," says Professor Kenneth Libbrecht. "Often the best way to understand a phenomenon is to try and reproduce it in the lab."

Professor Libbrecht and his colleagues use a vapor diffusion chamber, an insulated box kept at minus 40°C at the bottom and hot at the top, about 40°C. From a water source at the top, water vapor diffuses down, producing supersaturated air. The scientists put a wire into the chamber from below, and tiny ice crystals grow on the tip of the wire. By applying high voltage to the wire, the scientists make slender ice needles grow, with snow stars at each tip.

Along with awesome, mysterious beauty, snow can bring death and destruction—in the form of snowstorms and blizzards.

A snowstorm, according to the National Weather Service, entails six inches or more of heavy snow, ice accumulation, and dangerous wind chills. The service also issues winter storm warnings for lesser accumulations of snow accompanied by high winds. The term "blizzard" is reserved for falling or blowing snow accompanied by winds of 35 miles an hour or more, making for low visibility (less than a quarter of a mile for an extended period).

WHAT MAKES A SNOWSTORM?

Most large snowstorms begin when the jet stream pushes cold Arctic air south from Canada. When the cold air collides with warmer air masses, the warm air rises and cools, forming clouds that produce snow. At the edge of the storm, where the low pressure area meets a high pressure area, the difference in pressure—the pressure gradient—sets off high winds, which blow the snow and can turn the storm into a blizzard.

Many snowstorms that strike the middle Atlantic and New England states are Nor'easters. Typically, a low pressure area off the coast of the Carolinas, where the warm Gulf Stream waters lie closest to shore, gains strength and moves north, picking up warmth and moisture from the Atlantic. When the fast-moving, warm, moist air mass meets cold air off the coast between New York and New England, two things happen. The cold air turns the moisture into snow and dumps it over a large area, and a low pressure area forms as the warm air rises over the cold. The low pressure area, spinning counterclockwise, sucks in winds from the northeast, giving the storm its name.

An Iowa newspaper first used the term "blizzard" to describe a severe snowstorm in the 1870s. Before that time, the word was used only to describe canon shots or volleys of musket fire. But severe snowstorms and blizzards have occurred regularly throughout American history. George Washington and Thomas Jefferson both kept weather journals, and each man reported three feet of snow—at Mount Vernon and Monticello, respectively—in January 1772. The snowstorm trapped both men in their homes, and is known to meteorologists as "the Washington and Jefferson Snowstorm." Washington's diary for January 27 reads "A snow which began in the night … kept constantly at it the whole day with the wind hard & cold from the northward." The next day he wrote: "The same snow continued all last night and all this day with equal violence the wind being very cold and hard from the northward— drifting the snow into high banks."

The day after Christmas in 1778, with the country in the grip of the Revolutionary War, a major snowstorm hit the East Coast, blanketing the country from New Jersey to southern

Traffic sits immobilized in Buffalo, New York, in November 2000. That winter, 159 inches of snow fell on the city, most of it lake-effect snow, which occurs when cold air crosses relatively warm water and piles snow on the leeward shore.

LAKE-EFFECT SNOW

"Lake-effect" snow, which regularly blankets large areas of the inland eastern United States and Canada, has its genesis in dry Arctic air. In fall and winter, the water in the Great Lakes becomes much warmer than the surrounding air. As the Arctic air blows down from Canada over the Great Lakes, and some other large lakes, the bottom layer of the air mass picks up some of the water's moisture and warmth. Since this parcel of air is now lighter than the air above it, it rises and cools. The moisture in the air condenses into droplets or ice crystals, forming clouds that travel with the wind toward the lee shore. Once over the land, the wind-driven clouds slow and pile up, or converge, dropping large amounts of snow.

That's why such cities as Buffalo, Rochester, and Syracuse, New York; Erie, Pennsylvania; Muskegon, Michigan; and South Bend, Indiana—all of which lie on or near the downwind sides of the Great Lakes—consistently set snow records.

Shown at left in a dark shade, clear, dry air moving eastward from Wisconsin picks up moisture as it crosses Lake Michigan. Dense clouds on the eastern shore of the lake indicate snow, which will fall on the lake's lee side.

New England. Meteorologists who reconstructed the event believe that a very cold air mass moving south from Canada—a high pressure system—clashed with a warm, humid air mass spinning counterclockwise over the still relatively warm seas off southern New England, a low pressure system. The warm air moved up over the cold air, producing snow, and the pressure differential resulted in high winds. On December 26, 18 inches of snow were recorded at Newport, Rhode Island, and the winds whipped the snow into drifts as high as 20 feet. Low visibility caused 28 ships to run aground on New York's Staten Island, and soldiers in both the Continental and British Armies froze to death in the bitter cold. Nine Hessian mercenaries, who were occupying Rhode Island, were found frozen at their posts, giving the event its nickname, "The Hessian Storm."

The notorious "Blizzard of 1888" formed in similar fashion, with a warm air mass clashing with a cold one. The storm stalled over New York City on March 11, dumping 21 inches of snow. Gusts of wind reaching 70 miles an hour created 20-foot drifts, stranding New Yorkers in buildings or on elevated trains. Temperatures sank well below 0°F. The storm, sometimes called the "Great White Hurricane," paralyzed the East Coast from the Chesapeake Bay to Maine. Telegraph and telephone service stopped, and 200 ships were grounded. More than 400 people lost their lives, and property damage was estimated at $25 million.

In January 1922—150 years to the day of the Washington and Jefferson Storm—more than two feet of snow fell on Washington, D.C., causing a tragic loss of life that gave the event its name: "The Knickerbocker Snowstorm." The storm began in the evening on Friday, January 27, and continued for some 30 hours. Despite the fact that the city was virtually paralyzed,

the Knickerbocker Theatre opened on Saturday evening, January 28, for the showing of the silent film *Get-Rich-Quick Wallingford.* The film was nearly over when the organ music was almost drowned out by a groaning, cracking sound, followed by a deafening crash as steel beams split and the roof collapsed under the weight of the snow. Ninety-eight people were killed, and more than 130 were injured and trapped in the wreckage. General John "Black Jack" Pershing sent cavalry and artillery troops to the rescue, and a heroic telephone company operator called doctors from all over the city to the scene. A nearby store was converted to a hospital. According to a contemporary newspaper account: "A man came to the entrance, willing to fight his way in if necessary. He

On January 28, 1922, despite an on-going snowstorm, the Knickerbocker Theatre in Washington, D.C., opened its doors. As the silent movie ended, a groaning, cracking sound drowned out the organist. The roof collapsed under the snow's weight, killing 98 people.

was the husband of a young bride, who, with a girlfriend, had attended the theater. 'You can't hold me back,' he cried.... 'Mary's there, and she wants me with her.'"

A subsequent investigation faulted the contractor for installing the steel beams only two inches into the walls rather than the required eight inches. The architect of the theater, his career in ruins, later committed suicide.

The New England blizzard of 1978 began when the jet stream steered a low pressure mass from the Midwest—known as an Alberta Clipper—east toward the Atlantic. A high pressure system over the Atlantic blocked the storm from going out to sea. The difference in pressure caused gale-force winds, and snow fell for 36 hours. The winds, which reached speeds of more than 70 miles an hour, piled snow into drifts, blocking building entrances. Some 3,500 buried cars were found abandoned on highways and roads during the cleanup. Winds forced water up over land, causing coastal flooding. Some 10,000 people went to emergency shelters, and 2,500 houses were destroyed or seriously damaged. The blizzard claimed 54 lives, including that of ten-year-old Peter Gosselin. According to the *Providence Journal-Bulletin,* Peter was last seen playing in snow drifts near his home in Uxbridge, Massachusetts, at about noon on the second day of the blizzard. When he failed to return home, 3,000 people searched for him for three weeks. Later, a mail carrier noticed a mitten sticking out from a pile of snow a few feet from the Gosselins' front door. He pulled on the mitten and found the boy's frozen body.

The "Storm of the Century" struck the second week of March 1993, bringing hurricane force winds, tornadoes, and snow that fell as far south as Tallahassee, Florida, and as far

Rescue workers search for survivors and victims in the wreckage of the Knickerbocker Theatre. Its roof collapsed during a snowstorm in January 1922, trapping more than a hundred people under steel, wood, concrete, and plaster.

north as Canada's Maritime Provinces. Thirteen inches of snow fell on Birmingham, Alabama, setting a record, and 50 inches fell on North Carolina's Mount Mitchell. The storm formed when a cold polar air mass met warmer air, pushing it upward and creating a low pressure area near the ground. The surface air spiraled around the low pressure zone, producing a cyclone. The storm was blamed for more than 250 deaths, plus 48 people missing at sea as well as $3 to $6 billion in damages. During the blizzard, more than one-quarter of all flights in the United States were cancelled for two days.

The blizzard of January 1996 rivaled the Storm of the Century, breaking records for snow fall in some areas, notably Philadelphia, which saw 30.7 inches of snow, and New Jersey, whose all-time record snowfall of 35 inches was reached at Whitehouse Station. Although the Middle Atlantic states were most affected by the 1996 blizzard, the storm began in the Rockies. It traveled toward the Gulf of Mexico and then moved up the East Coast in the typical pattern of a Nor'easter. The warm, moist air from the south met a large, cold air mass that was firmly entrenched over the northeast. Temperatures in New England were below zero is some places, and the dense, cold air stalled the warm air as it tried to push northward, prolonging the snow and producing record snowfalls. In the aftermath of the storm, a warm spell caused rapid melting and floods forced thousands from their homes in parts of Ohio, Pennsylvania, West Virginia, New Jersey, Maryland, and New York.

FORECASTING SNOW

Although snow forecasts are improving, predicting snow and the amount of snowfall continues to challenge meteorologists.

"You have to forecast the development of a low pressure system that might not exist 12 hours beforehand—the development, not just the movement," explained Dr. Louis Uccellini, director of the National Centers for Environmental Prediction. "You have to forecast the structure of the cold and warm air. There's a fine line between rain and snow

U.S. RAIN, SNOW, AND DROUGHT RECORDS

Most rain in 24 hours:	43 inches in Alvin, Texas, July 25-26, 1979
Maximum annual rainfall:	704.83 inches in Kukui, Hawaii, 1982
Least annual rainfall:	None at all in Death Valley, California, 1929
Longest dry period:	767 days—from October 3, 1912, to November 8, 1914, in Bagdad, California
Most snow in 24 hours:	75.8 inches in Silver Lake, Colorado, April 14-15, 1921
Maximum seasonal snow:	1,140 inches at the Mount Baker Ski Area in Washington, 1998-1999
Maximum snow depth:	451 inches in Tamarack, California, March 11, 1911

according to the vertical distribution of the temperature. And you have to forecast moisture. Any one of those is hard to forecast in themselves. And, although the storm may be over a very large area, snow may fall only in a relatively small area."

Unlike most other weather systems, snowstorms come in relatively narrow bands. The bands are formed either by a mechanism called symmetric instability, parallel rows of rising and falling air, or by topography (for instance, when a storm pushes winds against a mountain, a band of snow may form parallel to the mountain). As a result of these bands, snowfall can vary widely in a relatively small area—even within the same city. Meteorologists hope that onging study of the structure of snow bands will improve snow forecasting.

Seen from space, the March 1993 "Storm of the Century" zeroes in on the mid-Atlantic coast. The cyclonic storm packed hurricane-force winds, tornadoes, and heavy snowfall in a one-two-three punch.

THE RESTLESS WIND:

AIR ON THE MOVE

"The answer is blowin' in the wind."
BOB DYLAN, 1963

A breeze puffs up sails, sending boats skimming across a rippling bay. A strong wind topples an old oak, which crashes onto a roof. A windstorm turns umbrellas inside out and makes pedestrians hold onto their hats.

Defined as "the flow of air relative to the Earth's surface," wind is energy on the move. It can be fierce, a hurricane, or it can be gentle, a soft breeze on a summer night. It pushes weather systems from place to place; without wind there would be few changes in the weather.

How does wind work?

Radiant energy rises from the Earth's surface. When it reaches the tropopause, the top of the troposphere, it cannot go any higher and moves horizontally. Heated air moves toward the Poles, while colder air moves in to replace it. The circulating air masses create differences in pressure. The pressure gradient force, the difference in pressure across distances, pushes air from high pressure areas to areas of low pressure. The greater the pressure difference, the stronger the wind.

Dandelion seeds waft in a soft wind. Wind, the horizontal movement of air, propagates plants, powers sailboats and windmills, takes kites to towering heights, and cools torrid summer nights.

Jet streams steer storms. The polar jet stream sometimes dives south in the winter, causing cold snaps. Or it can retreat north, letting us bask in unusually warm winter weather.

Within the jet streams are segments of even faster moving air known as jet streaks. These bundles of strong wind reach speeds higher than 160 knots. The atmosphere has to adjust to the extra energy generated by jet streaks, and it does so by forcing air up or down on either side of the streak. These rising and falling air pockets help determine where storms develop.

HIGHS, LOWS, AND MONSOONS

When air piles up in the upper atmosphere, it is forced to sink, creating an area of high pressure near the surface. In the Northern Hemisphere, air is forced clockwise around high pressure systems. The high pressure area itself enjoys sunny days with little rain. The air spiraling around the high pressure area usually brings northerly winds and cold air to the

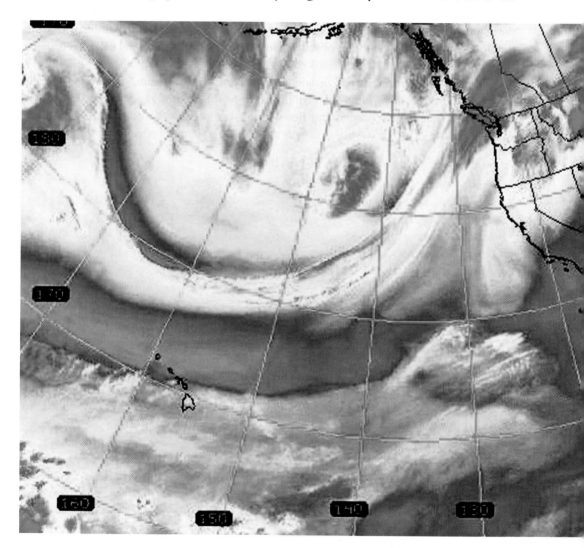

In the Northern Hemisphere, the polar jet stream blows west to east, shifting north and south with the seasons. In North America, the jet stream usually hovers above the U.S.-Canadian border.

area east of the high pressure and brings southerly winds with warm air to the west.

The Bermuda High, for example, is a high pressure ridge that breaks off from the Azorean or Atlantic High in summer. The high centers over the very warm waters of the Gulf Stream and brings long periods of warm, humid air to the eastern United States.

Monsoon winds are caused by differences in temperature between landmasses and oceans. The waters surrounding India and Southeast Asia stay at much the same temperatures all year around, but the land temperatures change with the seasons. In the Northern Hemisphere summer, the landmass grows much hotter than the oceans. The area above the ground expands and creates a low pressure area. A moisture-laden wind from the ocean— the southwest monsoon—is drawn into the low pressure area of India and Southeast Asia, bringing rain. In the winter, the land cools and the less dense air over the warmer sea draws a cool wind from the land, the northeast monsoon.

The term "monsoon" comes from an Arabic word for "seasons," and is usually used to describe changing wind conditions in India and Southeast Asia. But shifting monsoonal winds are also found in Africa, Australia, Central America, and North America.

North America's monsoon develops in early summer as intensifying sunlight heats dry inland areas in the southwestern United States and Mexico. Rising warm air over Mexico's Sierra Madre and Central Plateau pulls moisture from the Atlantic and Pacific Oceans and the Gulfs of Mexico and California. The hot, moist air dumps heavy rain over the arid plains of Mexico and the southwestern U.S. as far north as Colorado.

Farmers, ranchers, water resource managers, and firefighting agencies depend on these quenching rains, and scientists in the United States and Mexico are working together on a large-scale study of the North American monsoon.

"A long-term goal of the project is to produce forecasts of the monsoon's onset with perhaps more than a week of lead time," said researcher David Gochis of the National Center for Atmospheric Research in Boulder, Colorado.

BOUNDARY LAYER AND KATABATIC WINDS

Near the ground, in the boundary layer, which extends up to about a mile above the Earth's surface, the winds are influenced by topography. The Earth's surface exerts a frictional drag on winds near its surface, and sometimes slows the wind. That's why winds crossing oceans and deserts usually blow faster than winds that have to go around hills and trees. CONTINUED ON PAGE 124

ON THE FOLLOWING PAGES: **The southwest monsoon, a moisture-laden wind from the ocean, lashes the Indian subcontinent with rain during the summer, when the landmass grows hotter than the surrounding waters.**

ON PAGES 122-123: **An August monsoon descends on Arizona. Monsoons develop as intensifying sunlight heats the Earth and rising air pulls moisture from the sea, triggering intense rains.**

....

When the wind increases speed by at least three steps on the Beaufort Scale—about 16 knots—and sustains that speed for about a minute, meteorologists call the phenomenon a squall. Squalls often occur along the line of a cold front and are accompanied by a roll-shaped horizontal cloud.

If you listen to a weather forecast in a place far from home, you may hear some unfamiliar wind names. Regional winds can have strong local weather consequences, and people in the areas affected by them usually know the names well. Many of these winds are katabatic winds, from a Greek word meaning "going downhill."

Katabatic winds come in two varieties: hot and cold. Warm, dry katabatic winds—sometimes referred to as foehn winds—lose moisture when they climb over a mountain range. The dehydrated wind moves down the leeward slope, and the pressure around it compresses it. The compression increases the temperature of the air and, as it heats up, the air expands—or tries to. Sometimes it is forced through valleys or passes. As the air travels, it gains speed and temperature and loses humidity, sometimes raising temperatures as much as 50°F in a short period. The Chinook winds, for example, climb over the Rocky Mountains, dumping precipitation. The dehydrated, heated-up winds descend the eastern slopes of the mountain range and tumble onto the Great Plains. Other examples of these warm, dry winds include the zonda winds in Argentina, the No'wester in New Zealand, the hamsin in the Middle East, the Diablo winds around San Francisco, and the Santa Ana winds in southern California.

The hot, dry winds are said to raise tensions and exert evil influences on people who experience them. Mystery writer Raymond Chandler immortalized this "Santa Ana condition" in the novel *Red Wind*: "There was a desert wind blowing that night. It was one of those hot, dry Santa Anas that come down through the mountain passes and curl your hair and make your skin itch and your nerves jump. On nights like that every booze party ends in a fight. Meek little wives feel the edge of a carving knife and study their husbands' necks."

The Santa Ana winds do more that roil tempers—they also spread wildfires, turning dry California hills into raging infernos.

Cold katabatic winds occur when air is cooled over a high, snow-covered mountain range and driven down the leeward slope by gravity, picking up speed. As the air descends, it warms, but still remains cool relative to its surroundings. One example of this cool wind is the mistral, in southern France. In winter and spring, air cooled over France's Massif Central and the Pyrenees flows down into the Garonne and Rhone Valleys, which funnel the wind south toward the Mediterranean. The mistral spreads cold winds over southern France and as far as North Africa and Italy. Similar cool katabatic winds include the Bora in the Adriatic and the Oroshi in Japan.

HARNESSING THE WIND

Humans have long utilized the wind's energy. Before the age of steam, wind power propelled ships. The Persians pioneered windmills for grinding grain and CONTINUED ON PAGE 130

A string of thunderstorms, or squall line, hovers over the Atlantic Ocean just southeast of Bermuda. Squall lines mark the replacement of warm, moist air with cooler, drier air and can trigger intense storms with high winds.

ON THE FOLLOWING PAGES: **A hamsin, a hot, dry wind from the east that blows on average 50 days a year, carries desert sand into Riyadh, Saudi Arabia, choking traffic and filling the air with thick dust.**

ON PAGES 128-129: **Rainless summers set the stage for wildfires in southern California every autumn, and Santa Ana winds whip the smallest spark into a frenzy of destruction, as seen here near San Diego, October 2003.**

pumping water, and the Dutch improved the design.

Although steam and fossil-fuel power superseded it, wind power is making a comeback. Wind farms, or power plants that use turbines to turn wind energy into electricity and mechanical power, have sprouted in 30 U.S. states as well as in Europe and India.

The wind turns the wing-shaped blades of giant turbines, which turn a shaft. Eventually, the energy reaches a generator, which converts it into electricity. According to the American Wind Energy Association, a typical turbine can provide about 10,000 kilowatt hours of energy each year—enough to power the average household.

Since wind will keep being generated as long as the sun shines down on Earth, it is a renewable energy source—unlike fossil fuels. Also unlike fossil fuels, wind power doesn't pollute the air or contribute to global warming.

OTHER REGIONAL WINDS

Elephanta	A strong southerly or southeasterly wind that blows on the west coast of India. Its appearance marks the end of the southwest monsoon.
Haboob	A strong wind that stirs up sandstorms in the Sudan.
Norther or Blue Norther	A cold, strong northerly wind that sweeps across the southern Great Plains as far as Texas, sending the thermometer plummeting.
Papagayo	A violent northeasterly wind that whips the Pacific coast of Central America in the autumn. It is actually part of a norther that has crossed the mountains of Central America.
Pineapple Express	A southwest wind that brings warm, humid air across the Pacific from Hawaii to the Pacific Northwest and California often triggering heavy rains.
Shamal	This wind blows northwesterly over Iraq and the Persian Gulf during the summer. It usually decreases in strength after sunset.
Sirocco	Also called scirocco or jugo, this wind begins in North Africa when low pressure cells pick up the hot, dry air blowing up from the Sahara. When this air mass meets the cooler, more humid air over the Mediterranean, fronts develop, bringing rain, high winds and thunderstorms. When the wind reaches the European coast, it delivers rain. The Sirocco may prove the adage that "an ill wind blows nobody good": It brings hot, dry winds and blowing sand to North Africa, storms to the Mediterranean, and cold, wet weather to Europe.
Squamish	A wind made from cold polar air that funnels into some of the fjords of British Columbia.
Williwaw	The name given to winds that blast down from the mountains to the sea in the Aleutian Islands or the Straits of Magellan.

THE ANSWER IS BLOWING IN THE WIND....

Where was the strongest gust of wind recorded?

At Mount Washington Observatory in New Hampshire on April 12, 1934: 231 mph. More recently, on May 3, 1999, a Doppler on Wheels clocked winds of 301 mph in a tornado in Oklahoma City, Oklahoma.

What is the most consistently windy place in the world?

Port Martin, Antarctica, where, in 1951, winds averaged 40 mph throughout the year.

Mount Washington Observatory (top) in New Hampshire may have measured the strongest wind gust (in 1934), but Antarctica and its denizens (above) deal with the most consistent strong winds—in 1951, they averaged 40 mph.

Wind turbines rise against a dark sky west of Wilhelms-
haven, Germany. Wind power is the world's fastest growing
forms of energy technology, and wind farms are sprouting in
Europe, Asia, and the United States.

But wind farms are not without controversy. For example, some environmentalists and local residents are battling a 23-square-mile wind farm developers propose to build off the coast of Cape Cod. The proposed 130 wind turbines would rise 420 feet above the surface of the sea—100 feet higher than the Statue of Liberty—about five miles offshore.

Supporters say the project will reduce pollution, global warming, and dependence on foreign oil, while opponents cite danger to seabirds, harm to tourism, interference with commercial and sports fishing, obstructed views, and visual pollution.

"This project is for a good purpose—increased alternative energy—but it is in the wrong place," said Guy Martin, an attorney who represents Cape Cod residents opposed to the offshore wind farm.

THE BEAUFORT SCALE

How strong are the winds? Ask Admiral Beaufort. Sir Francis Beaufort devised a wind force scale while commanding the *Woolwich*, a 44-gun man-of-war. For example, #1 was described as "just sufficient to give steerage way." By 1838, it was mandatory for all log entries in the British Navy. Still in use, the scale has been adapted as shown below:

Beaufort number	Wind speed in knots	Description
0	less than 1	calm
1	1 - 3	light air
2	4 - 6	light breeze
3	7 - 10	gentle breeze
4	11 - 16	moderate breeze
5	17 - 21	fresh breeze
6	22 - 27	strong breeze
7	28 - 33	near gale
8	34 - 40	gale
9	41 - 47	strong gale
10	48 - 55	storm
11	56 - 63	violent storm
12	greater than or equal to 64	hurricane

WIND SHEAR AND MICROBURSTS

Wind shear is a sudden and drastic change in wind direction or speed over a short distance.

Wind usually travels horizontally. But during thunderstorms and frontal passages wind can take a vertical direction. Violent downward air blasts, called microburst wind shear, can cause airplanes to lose lift and crash. Planes are especially vulnerable during takeoffs and landings, when their slower speeds and proximity to the ground make correction difficult. Since 1996, all U.S. airliners are equipped with devices that warn of possible wind shear.

STORMY WEATHER:
SEVERE THUNDERSTORMS AND TORNADOES

*"Don't know why,
there's no sun up in the sky,
Stormy weather."*

"STORMY WEATHER," TED KOEHLER AND HAROLD ARLEN, 1933

The dictionary defines a storm as "an atmospheric disturbance manifested in strong winds accompanied by rain, snow, or other precipitation and often by thunder and lightning."

But that does not begin to describe some of the calamitous storms that have torn across the globe throughout history, and that do billions of damage each year: thunderstorms, blizzards, tornadoes, hurricanes.

For a crash course in storms, look at the superstorm that delivered tornadoes, hurricane-force winds, and blizzards to a wide swath of the United States and Canada during the second week of March 1993.

Hurricane-strength winds—peaking at 99 miles an hour—raced across the Gulf Coast, bringing walls of water as high as 12 feet, swamping boats, smashing cars, and ripping houses from their foundations. At the same time, snow fell on Tallahassee and the Florida Panhandle. Lightning streaked across the sky, and a squall line—followed closely by a cold front—sped across Florida, bringing rain, gale-force winds, and 27 tornadoes. Meanwhile, air pressure dropped to the lowest levels ever recorded in places from the Carolinas to Canada's Maritime Provinces. Heavy

A supercell thunderstorm, a storm with a deep, rotating updraft, menaces the Texas plain. The severest of thunderstorms, a supercell can produce strong downbursts of rain and hail and lead to flash floods and tornadoes.

snows bombarded the East Coast, and fierce winds whipped it into a frenzy, piling up drifts and reducing visibility. Twenty-six states—from Texas to the Ohio Valley to Maine—reported heavy damages, and 270 people died.

What makes a storm?

The essential ingredients are moisture, or water vapor, in the lower atmosphere and colder air up above. But each kind of storm develops in its own way.

THUNDERSTORMS

Thunderstorms occur when an updraft of warm, moisture-laden air rises quickly and hits the higher, colder air two or three miles above the ground, causing instability. As the package of air rises, some of the water vapor turns into clouds. The clouds grow upward, and the water vapor at the top of the clouds freezes. Precipitation—rain and, sometimes, hail—falls, creating downdrafts. This updraft-downdraft combination is known as a storm cell.

Right now—and at any given moment—some 1,800 thunderstorms are in progress across the globe. They range from single-cell storms, consisting of one pair of up and down drafts linked in a convective loop, to supercell thunderstorms, which have deep, rotating updrafts. Single-cell storms usually last no more than half an hour and do little damage, while supercell storms can generate extreme weather, including hail, flash floods, and tornadoes.

All thunderstorms include lightning. Updrafts of air carry water droplets, which are electrically charged, up to heights where some of the water freezes and clouds form. In the process, the positive and negative charges get separated, with the negative charges dropping to the bottom of the cloud. The positive and negative charges react within the cloud, discharging electrical energy. The negative charge at the bottom of the cloud prompts a positive charge to rise on the ground. When the two powerfully attractive charges connect, we see the clash as a lightning flash.

Lightning, in turn, creates thunder, by heating the air to more than 43,000°F. The superheated air expands very quickly and contracts just as quickly as it cools after the flash. This fast expansion and contraction sets air molecules moving back and forth, creating sound waves. The rumbling sound we hear is due to the fact that the sound waves have to reach us from different points on the lightning flash.

Lightning not only kills people, it does several hundred million dollars in damage to property and forests each year, according to the National Weather Service. In addition, thunderstorms can trigger flash floods, which cause 140 deaths a year and inflict some $2 billion in property damages. Winds generated by thunderstorms can damage buildings, blow down power lines, and endanger aircraft. And hail pelted down during thunderstorms causes extensive damages to crops, homes, and cars.

LIGHTNING KILLS

Around the globe, lightning strikes the ground about 100 times every second. In the U.S, lightning kills an average of nearly a hundred people a year and causes some 500 injuries. After floods and flash floods, lightning is the biggest weather killer in the U.S. The National Weather Services urges people to avoid lightning hazards by obeying the "30-30" rule. When you see lightning, count the seconds until you hear thunder. If the time is 30 seconds or less, go to a safe place.

Naked electrical energy, jagged bolts of lightning strike an
Arizona hillside. Negative charges at the bottom of a thun-
dercloud prompt a positive charge to rise from the ground.
The collision of the attractive charges is seen as lightning.

HAIL:
THE RECORD
HOLDERS

According to the National Climate Extremes Committee, a hailstone found in a bean field in Aurora, Nebraska, on June 22, 2003, is the biggest ever recovered in the United States (see below). The icy mass had a diameter of 7 inches and measured 18.75 inches around.

The Aurora stone was, however, outweighed by the former champion, a hail chunk that fell on Coffeyville, Kansas, on September 3, 1970. Long hailed as the record holder, the Coffeyville stone weighed in at 1.65 pounds.

Small wonder that hail collectors generally don hard hats. Where are the record stones now? They were kept for a short time at the National Center for Atmospheric Research in Boulder, Colorado, but were then sliced up so scientists could study them.

Hail leaves a calling card in the form of shattered glass on the windshield of a car in western Kansas. The Great Plains states east of the Rocky Mountains get the most hail, usually during the summer.

Hail is born several miles above the ground, within the huge cumulonimbus clouds known as thunderheads. The high-altitude, below-freezing temperatures of the cloud supercool the moisture inside. Droplets of supercooled water collide with ice pellets within the cloud and freeze to them. Instead of precipitating out of the cloud right away, the ice pellets are kept aloft by the strong updraft associated with the storm, giving them time to grow bigger and bigger. When they fall to the lower level of a cloud, they melt but they refreeze as rising air pushes them to higher levels, growing in bulk. Finally, when these chunks grow so heavy that the updraft can no longer hold them, they fall to the ground.

Hail tends to fall in swaths ranging from a few square acres to much larger areas. The chunks within these swaths are sometimes piled so deep they have to be removed with snowplows. Hail can fall anytime, anywhere, but in the United States, it is most prevalent during the summer in the Great Plains states east of the Rocky mountains, especially in the area where Colorado, Nebraska, and Wyoming meet—a place nicknamed "Hail Alley." Parts of China, India, and Europe also experience frequent damaging hailstorms.

In the United States, hail inflicts nearly $1 billion in damage to property and crops each year. A single hailstorm that occurred in Denver, Colorado, in July 1990 caused $625 million in damage, mainly to cars and the roofs of buildings. During that same storm, 47 people were trapped in an amusement park Ferris wheel, when the power failed, and were pelted with softball-sized hail.

A 2002 summer storm dropped tennis ball-size chunks of hail on Italy's lucrative wine growing area, destroying most of the grapes just before harvesttime and causing some $200 million in damages to the grapes, olives, and other crops. But a hailstorm that struck Munich, Germany, in July 1984 holds the Guinness World Record for the worst hailstorm damage toll. The hail destroyed crops, stripped the bark from trees, and damaged 70,000 roofs and 250,000 cars. Some 400 people were injured, and property damage totaled an estimated $1 billion.

When a tornado swept through the fictional Kansas farm where Dorothy lived with her Auntie Em in the 1939 film *The Wizard of Oz,* the spiraling vortex transported the heroine to a magical kingdom "somewhere over the rainbow." Nonfiction tornadoes, though less romantic, are equally dramatic. Farmer Will Keller gave the following eyewitness account of a June 1928 tornado that tore through Greensburg, Kansas:

"The family had entered the cellar, and I was in the doorway just about to enter and close the door when I decided that I would take a last look at the approaching tornado.... Suddenly the tornado came on, the end gradually rising above the ground. I could have stood there only a few seconds, but so impressed was I with what was going on it seemed a long time. At last the great shaggy end of the funnel hung directly overhead. Everything was as still as death. There was a strong gassy odor and it seems that I could not breathe. There was a screaming, hissing sound coming directly from the end of the funnel. I looked up and, to my astonishment I saw right up into the heart of the tornado. There was a circular opening in the center of the funnel, about 50 or 100 feet in diameter, and extending straight upward for a distance of at least one half mile, as best I could judge under the circumstances. The walls of this opening were of rotating clouds and the whole was made brilliantly visible by constant flashes of lightning which zigzagged from side to side.... Around the lower rim of the great vortex, small tornadoes were constantly forming and breaking away. These looked like tails and they writhed their way around the end of the funnel. It was these that made the hissing noise. I noticed that the direction of rotation of the great whirl was anticlockwise, but the small twisters rotated both ways...."

CONTINUED ON PAGE 148

Tornadoes such as this one in Kansas, May 2004, form in supercell thunderstorms when unstable air starts to rotate. Updrafts near the ground change the rotation from horizontal to vertical, creating a funnel with high winds inside.

ON THE FOLLOWING PAGES: **This tornado tearing across Oklahoma farmland was rated F3. F3 tornadoes feature winds blowing 150 to 206 miles an hour and inflict severe damage, including tearing roofs off houses, uprooting trees, and tossing cars into the air.**

ON PAGES 144-145: **Ruined homes, scattered furnishings, and storm-tossed vehicles litter a street in Oklahoma City, Oklahoma, after a tornado hit on May 3, 1999. More than 70 tornadoes were reported in Oklahoma, Kansas, and northern Texas that day.**

INSIDE A VIOLENT STORM

....

S trong winds flowing over weaker winds can cause the air in between to spin on a horizontal axis, like a pencil rolling along a table (small diagram, below). When a vigorous updraft ingests the spinning air, its rotation tilts toward the vertical and causes the updraft to rotate. Without such rotation no thunderstorm can produce a tornado.

Upper Level Winds

Updraft

Wind Shear

Middle Level winds

Rear Flank Updraft

Why does one thunderstorm and not another produce a tornado? It depends on how surrounding winds interact with the storm's updraft, the flow of warm, moist air that rises up its core. When the updraft is strong, air being drawn into the storm may surge upward as fast as 100 miles an hour to heights of ten miles or more. This rising column of air will rotate if surrounding winds vary sharply in speed or direction from lower to higher levels. Such a rotating updraft, called a mesocyclone, is the parent circulation of large tornadoes.

Only about half of all mesocyclones, however, produce tornadoes. When they do, the twister usually appears on the storm's rear side, near where a stream of

cool air from the rear-flank downdraft spins into the warm main inflow. Drawing upon the strength of the mesocyclone, the tornado may extend upward through the storm for several miles. Only the most violent last for more than a few tens of minutes.

Scientists who scan thunderstorms with Doppler radar report that mesocyclones may appear as much as 20 minutes before tornadoes, offering far more accurate, timely warnings.

As many as half a dozen smaller twisters may form inside some large ones (right). Low pressure at ground level creates a strong downdraft at the center of the vortex. Secondary vortices then form as downward flowing air meets air rushing into the tornado. Because these smaller twisters also revolve around the rim of the main one, they often leave complex damage paths.

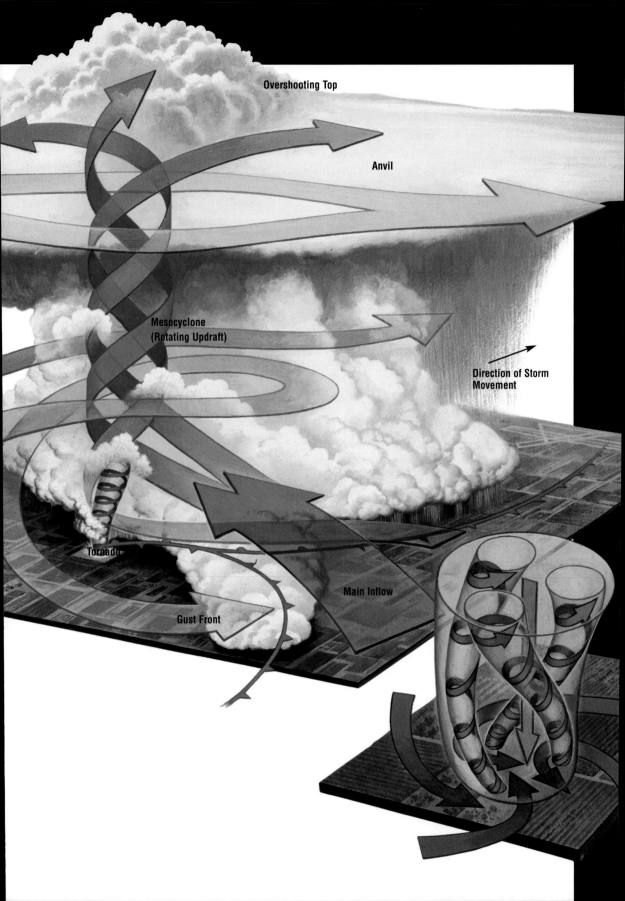

Overshooting Top

Anvil

Mesocyclone
(Rotating Updraft)

Direction of Storm
Movement

Tornado

Main Inflow

Gust Front

the opening was completely hollow except for something I could not exactly make out, but suppose it was a detached wind cloud. This thing was in the center and was moving up and down."

Farmer Keller was in the right place to see tornadoes. Kansas sits smack in the middle of "Tornado Alley." Although meteorologists stress that tornadoes can occur anywhere, they are most common in this broad sweep of the Midwest. According to the American Meteorological Society's *Glossary of Weather and Climate,* Tornado Alley "encompasses the great lowland areas of the Mississippi, the Ohio, and lower Missouri River Valleys. Although no state is entirely free of tornadoes, they are most frequent in the Plains area between the Rocky Mountains and Appalachians."

This swath of the country has all the ingredients for making tornadoes. Warm, humid air blows in from the Gulf of Mexico, and hot, dry air comes down from the Rockies. Winds from the east form a layer of colder air above the warmer air. This layer acts as a lid, or cap, on the warmer air below, which cannot rise and dissipate its energy as rain. Instead, the energy builds to pressure-cooker strength.

RATING TORNADOES ON THE F SCALE

In the 1970s, Dr. Tetsuya "Ted" Fujita, a Japanese-born meteorologist who taught at the University of Chicago, devised a scale that links wind speeds to the actual damage done by the tornado. Although Professor Fujita specified 12 classifications, any tornado above F5 would be unthinkable. Just after the April 1974 outbreak, Professor Fujita mapped each tornado, classifying each on a scale from F0 to F5.

Here is the Fujita scale now used by the National Weather Service:

Scale	Wind Estimatein MPH	Typical Damage
F0	<73	Light damage. Some damage to chimneys and signboards; branches broken off; shallow-rooted trees pushed over.
F1	73 - 112	Moderate damage. Surfaces peeled off roofs; mobile homes pushed off foundations or overturned; moving cars blown off roads.
F2	113 - 157	Considerable damage. Roofs torn off frame houses; mobile homes demolished; large trees snapped or uprooted; light-object missiles generated; cars lifted off ground.
F3	158 - 206	Severe damage. Roofs and some walls torn off well-constructed houses; trains overturned; most trees in forest uprooted; heavy cars lifted off ground and thrown.
F4	207 - 260	Devastating damage. Well-constructed houses leveled; structures with weak foundations blown some distance; cars thrown; large missiles generated.
F5	261 - 318	Incredible damage. Strong frame houses leveled off foundations; automobile-size missiles fly through the air in excess of 109 yards; trees debarked.

(Wind speeds are approximate; different wind speeds may cause similar damage.)

Tornadoes begin with a thunderstorm—usually a supercell storm. Winds near the ground change direction and speed up as they rise, producing an invisible horizontal spinning in the lower atmosphere. Moist air near the ground rises, forming an updraft. Sucked into the updraft, the spinning air becomes a strong rotation. As the storm heats up, it draws air cooled and moistened by rain into the updraft. The cool, humid air condenses, forming a "wall cloud" inside the cycling air. Scientists are not sure exactly how, but something shapes this rotating air into a funnel that spins down to Earth. The winds inside the funnel reach speeds as high as 300 mph, turning any object in their path into a deadly projectile. The winds send cars airborne, rip homes to pieces, and turn the pieces into lethal missiles. Because this column focuses destructive energy on a relatively small target (typically a path 50 to several hundred yards wide that runs about one or two miles) in a short time (most tornadoes last less than ten minutes) tornadoes are considered nature's most violent storms.

The deadliest U.S. tornado, the Tri-State Tornado of March 18, 1925, killed 695 people in a spree that cut a 219-mile path of destruction through Missouri, Illinois, and Indiana. In Murphysboro, Illinois, alone, the tornado claimed 234 lives—a record for the most tornado fatalities in a single city or town.

On April 3 and 4, 1974, the worst tornado outbreak in U.S. history exploded on the scene. In a 16-hour nightmare, 147 tornadoes touched down in 13 states—Alabama, Georgia, Illinois, Indiana, Kentucky, Michigan, Mississippi, North Carolina, Ohio, South Carolina, Tennessee, Virginia, and West Virginia—and another hit Windsor, Ontario. Seven tornadoes were rated F5; 23 were rated F4. Casualties included more than 300 deaths and more than 5,000 people injured. Damage was estimated at $600 million. (Risk Management Solutions, Inc., estimates that if the 1974 tornado outbreak were repeated today, the cost to the U.S. insurance industry could reach as high as $3.5 billion for wind losses alone.) All together, the tornadoes carved a path of destruction more than 2,000 miles long. Worst hit was Xenia, Ohio, which suffered 34 deaths and $100 million in damages.

Dr. Ted Fujita, shown here with a tornado simulator in his lab at the University of Chicago, devised the Fujita, or F, scale system for measuring tornado strength. He also discovered microbursts and their link to plane crashes.

Shortly after the first federal weather forecast service began in 1870, under the U.S. Army Signal Corps, one Sgt. John P. Finley organized a team of 2,000 reporters to document tornadoes in the central and eastern United States. Using data from these observers, Sergeant Finley put together maps of tornado-triggering weather patterns and issued tornado alerts. But Finley's superiors in the Signal Corps thought these alerts provoked public panic. Even after the Weather Bureau took over from the Signal Corps, the word "tornado" was forbidden in forecasting. But as more scientific information about tornadoes became known, this policy gradually changed. The first documented successful forecast of a tornado came in 1948, when Air Force meteorologists Robert Miller and Ernest Fawbush, noting similarities in a developing weather pattern to a pattern that had produced a tornado a few days before, advised their superiors that another tornado threatened to hit Tinker Air Force Base in central Oklahoma. Emergency procedures were undertaken. Airplanes were secured, and people were warned to stay out of dangerous places. When the tornado hit—at 6 p.m. on March 25, 1948—damage was minimized and no one was hurt. Two years later, the National Weather Service officially revoked the ban on the word "tornado."

SKYWARN

"Skywarn" is an umbrella term for the network of storm spotters who report to their local National Weather Service Forecast Office or to local emergency management offices. National Weather Service meteorologists train volunteers in what to look for and how to stay safe.

To find out about volunteer opportunities in your area, call your local National Weather Service Forecast Office, which is listed in the blue pages of your telephone book, or go to www. srh.weather.gov. Click on the area of the map where you live, and you will be transferred to your local forecast office. Click on "Skywarn" to find out about openings and training classes.

Today, the National Weather Service's Storm Prediction Center in Norman, Oklahoma, uses state-of-the-art equipment and a vast store of weather knowledge to predict tornadoes. Meteorologists at the center look for temperature and wind patterns in the atmosphere that can supply the ingredients needed for a tornado: moisture, instability, lift, and wind shear. They use computer models and real-time observations from satellites, weather stations, balloons, airplanes, wind profilers, and other instruments. But by far the most important instrument, say National Weather Service officials, is the human brain. Forecasters must use their knowledge, experience, and skills to sort out and interpret all available data.

And, despite all the sophisticated high-tech equipment, tornado forecasters also rely on a network of volunteer weather spotters.

"Volunteers are our last line of defense against the ravages of winter storms, tornadoes, severe thunderstorms, and other weather events," said Storm Prediction Center meteorologist Rick Smith, who helps train volunteer storm spotters. "There are tens of thousands of these volunteers nationwide. A lot of them are amateur radio operators, volunteer firemen, police officers; they have different areas of interest but they share a sense of public service. Even with the great leaps of technology we've made, we still need eyes and ears on the ground. Radar can tell us that a tornado might be there—but people on the ground can tell us if it's actually there."

Equipped with Doppler radar, the Mile High Radar dome sits in the shadow of the Rocky Mountains in Boulder, Colorado. Doppler radar allows meteorologists to pinpoint severe weather with great speed and accuracy.

After planting a weather probe in the path of an F4
tornado that just leveled Manchester, South Dakota,
storm chaser Tim Samaras rushes to safety.

In addition to people who work as volunteer storm spotters for the National Weather Service, there are people who pursue severe storms and tornadoes as a hobby—to learn about them, to photograph them, or just to get a closer look.

David Hoadley, one of the pioneers in the field, got hooked on storms when he was a 17-year-old growing up in Bismarck, North Dakota.

"I had gone to the movies, but I could hear the thunder outside," he recalled. "My Dad knew where I usually sat, and he came to get me. 'There's a better show outside,' he said. There were big trees ripped out, and downed power lines were snapping in the wet grass like snakes."

Mr. Hoadley has been chasing storms ever since, missing only one year, while he was on his honeymoon. He analyzes weather patterns and plots the probable courses of storms on blank maps, then takes off in a car.

"I like to watch the complete cycle of a storm," he said. "The towering cumulus, the thunderstorm, the wall cloud with inflow bands at the base, then the tornado itself. Maybe there'll be more than one, if a gust front sweeps around it, so you want to drive to the east and southeast in case it triggers another. Finally, there are the golden clouds at sunset, drifting off toward the east. They're especially beautiful in eastern Colorado, where the sun goes down behind the mountains and turns the sky gold and lavender 'till the stars come out diamond bright. You look up at them and lose yourself wondering what's out there."

A retired government employee, Mr. Hoadley taught himself about weather. Another experienced and respected storm chaser, Dr. Chuck Doswell, is a meteorologist who has been chasing storms since he was a graduate student in 1972.

"I don't know why, but there's something about storms and tornadoes that fascinates me," he said. "The real experience is better than anything I ever imagined—it's dramatic, it's exciting, it's something very special. The fascination is with the motion. My most exciting chase? That's like asking me which of my children I love best. Each chase is unique, but one of the most exciting was the chase of a tornado in Pampa, Texas, on June 8, 1995. It was the first time I'd ever seen a tornado going through a town. There was a big funnel cloud with lots of debris. It was an F4 tornado, and we were relatively close—about a third of a mile—but not unsafe. We weren't in the path; it wasn't moving toward us. People say that a tornado sounds like a freight train, but I thought it sounded more like Niagara Falls."

WANT TO CHASE STORMS?

"The best way is to go with a reputable tour company," advises Dr. Doswell. "These tours were set up in response to the hype generated by the movie Twister. Tours are a good way to find out the reality of the experience rather than what you see on the silver screen. There's a lot of tedium. You're driving around a lot of the time, and staying in less than ideal motels. It's physically demanding, and there's no guarantee you'll see a tornado. But when and if you do, it's an experience you'll remember."

A number of tour companies sponsor organized chases in Tornado Alley each spring. Experienced storm chasers, usually meteorologists, brief guests each morning and lead them to places where exciting weather is predicted, and where they can watch and photograph developing storms at a safe distance. For information, go to www.tempesttours.com; www.silverliningtours.com; www.cloud9tours.com; or search under "storm chasing tours."

WATER-SPOUTS AND GUSTNADOES

Waterspouts are weak tornadoes that form over warm water—but they're strong enough to over-turn small boats and damage larger ships. Sailors off the east coast of Florida and the Keys often report waterspouts, but these non-supercell tornadoes also touch down on bays and lakes all over the world.

Gustnadoes are sometimes mistaken for tornadoes, but in actuality they are whirlwinds that form in thunderstorm outflows. They often have a spinning dust cloud at ground level—the reason for the confu-sion—but they do not connect with any cloud-based rotation.

A waterspout, a funnel with an intense vortex, reaches down to the South China Sea off the coast of Malaysia. These tornadoes over water, which often come in clusters, form when cooler air passes over warmer water.

When El Niño warms the ocean waters in the eastern tropical Pacific, the change in ocean temperatures causes the polar jet stream to shift south, bringing colder weather to the Midwest and Southeast. This cooler air may help suppress tornado activity in these parts of the country. But when La Niña causes the same ocean waters to grow colder, it also causes a shift in the subtropical jet stream. The subtropical jet shifts north, bringing warm air to the Midwest and Southeast, which feeds thunderstorms and increases the probability of tornadoes. A study conducted at Purdue University showed that El Niño and La Niña did not affect the total number of tornadoes in the United States, but they may be responsible for geographic shifts in tornado activity. The Purdue researchers found more tornadoes in the central and southern plains and the Gulf Coast during El Niño years. During La Niña years, tornado activity shifted to the lower Midwest, the Ohio and Tennessee Valleys, and the mid-Atlantic States. Many scientists believe that additional study on this possible correlation is needed.

TORNADO RECORDS IN THE UNITED STATES

- Record holder for path width is the F4 tornado that hit Hallam, Nebraska, on May 22, 2004. It cut a swath nearly two and a half miles wide. (Source: NOAA)

- The tornado with the biggest measured diameter touched down May 2, 1999, near Mulhall, Oklahoma. The University of Oklahoma's Doppler on Wheels calculated that the diameter inside the tornado measured 5,250 feet—just short of a mile. (Source: Guinness Book of World Records)

- The fastest tornado ever measured had winds of 301 mph. It was measured by a Doppler on Wheels on May 3, 1999, in Oklahoma City. (Source: Center for Severe Weather Research)

- Prize for the most tornadoes in a single month goes to May 2003, with 516 tornadoes reported and confirmed. (Source: NOAA)

- The tornado that hit central and northern Georgia on March 31, 1973, holds the record for cost. It ran up $1,250,000,000 in actual damages. (Source: NOAA)

- Oklahoma City, Oklahoma, has the dubious distinction of having been hit by the most tornadoes— more than 100. Huntsville, Alabama, is the runner up. (Source: NOAA)

- The year with the most tornadoes reported was 1973, which saw more than 1,100. (Source: NOAA)

- The highest elevation at which a tornado was observed is believed to be at 12,000 feet in Sequoia National Park, California, photographed by a hiker July 7, 2004. (Source: NOAA)

- The most tornado fatalities in a single city or town occurred during the Tri-State Tornado of March 18, 1925: At least 234 people died in Murphysboro, Illinois.

HURRICANES:
NATURE IN A RAGE

*"Queen of the Waves, look forth across the ocean
From north to south, from east to stormy west,
See how the waters with tumultuous motion
Rise up and foam without a pause or rest."*

"QUEEN OF THE WAVES," OLD FRENCH HYMN SUNG
AT ST. MARY'S ORPHAN ASYLUM DURING THE 1900 GALVESTON HURRICANE

Call it a hurricane, a typhoon, a cyclone, a willy-willy. Meteorologists lump them together under the term "tropical cyclone." By any of its names, this circulating weather system spells death and devastation. Small wonder that the word "hurricane" comes from the Carib Indian name "Hurican," the god of evil. The Caribs modeled their god after the Mayan god "Hurakan," who blew his breath across the churning water and brought forth dry land but later destroyed its inhabitants with a storm and a flood.

The first written European record of a hurricane was penned by none other than Christopher Columbus, who wrote in his log of a tropical cyclone on his second voyage, in 1494. Columbus may also have made the first hurricane forecast. In 1502, he warned the governor of Santo Domingo that a hurricane was approaching.

Hurricanes form over warm seas when water vapor condenses, releasing even more heat, fueling high winds and further lowering air pressure, creating a self-feeding meteorological monster.

Unfortunately, the forecast was ignored, and a Spanish treasure fleet set sail, got caught in the storm, and lost 20 ships and 500 men.

A tropical cyclone is an area of very low pressure around which winds flow—counter-clockwise in the Northern Hemisphere and clockwise in the Southern Hemisphere. Three ingredients are essential for making a tropical cyclone: warm tropical seas, moisture, and light winds above them. Let's look at how nature brews these ingredients into violent, destructive storms.

WEIGHING HURRICANES ON THE SAFFIR-SIMPSON SCALE

Meteorologists use a Category One to Five scale to estimate potential damage from a hurricane:

Category One   *Winds: 74 to 95 miles an hour. Storm surge: 4 to 5 feet above normal. Damage to unanchored mobile homes, shrubbery, trees, poorly constructed signs. Some coastal road flooding and pier damage. Notable hurricanes: Hurricane Allison, 1995; Hurricane Danny, 1997.*

Category Two   *Winds: 96 to 110 miles an hour. Storm surge: 6 to 8 feet above normal. Some damage to roofing, doors, and windows. Some trees blown down, and considerable damage to shrubbery. Considerable damage to homes, poorly constructed signs and piers. Flooding of coastal and low-lying roads. Small craft in unprotected waters break moorings. Notable hurricanes: Hurricane Bonnie, 1998; Hurricane George, 1998.*

Category Three   *Winds: 111 to 130 miles an hour. Storm surge: 9 to 12 feet above normal. Some structural damages to small houses and utility buildings. Foliage blown off trees and large trees blown down. Mobile homes and poorly constructed signs destroyed. Rising water cuts off low-lying escape routes three to five hours before the hurricane center arrives. Coastal flooding destroys small structures, and floating debris batters larger buildings. Low-lying land flooded eight or more miles inland. Notable hurricane: Hurricane Fran, 1996.*

Category Four   *Winds: 131 to 155 miles an hour. Storm surge: 13 to 18 feet above normal. Extensive roof damage to small houses. Shrubs, trees, and all signs blown down. Mobile homes completely destroyed. Extensive damage to doors and windows. Flooding may require evacuation as far inland as six miles. Notable hurricanes: Hurricanes Felix and Opal, 1995; Hurricane Ivan, 2004.*

Category Five   *Winds: greater than 155 miles an hour. Storm surge: generally greater than 18 feet above normal. Complete roof failure on many homes and industrial buildings. Small utility buildings blown over or away. All shrubs, trees, and signs blown down. Major damage to lower floors of all structures less than 15 feet above sea level and within 500 miles of shoreline. Notable hurricanes: Hurricane Mitch, 1998; Hurricane Andrew, 1992.*

With winds gusting up to 175 miles an hour, Hurricane Andrew rips through Coconut Grove, Florida, in the early morning hours of August 24, 1992. A Category Four hurricane, Andrew left some 250,000 people homeless.

The fishing boat *Delaware* rides out a storm in the Atlantic. Hurricanes and storms make commercial fishing one of the most dangerous occupations. In the U.S., the on-the-job death rate is 30 times the national average.

Before Ivan—Ivan the Terrible—became a Category Four hurricane that tore through the Caribbean and the Gulf Coast of the United States in 2004, it was an easterly wave blowing from Africa's Sahara. The temperature differences between the hot Sahara and the cooler air along the Gulf of Guinea coast create instability in the atmosphere. About 60 of these wavelike disturbances move westward with the tropical easterly winds each year. They are weak troughs of low pressure that sometimes intensify into tropical storms or hurricanes. About 85 percent of all major hurricanes originate as easterly waves, according to NOAA.

Warm summer temperatures in the tropical Atlantic provide the energy source that can turn easterly waves into tropical depressions, tropical storms, and hurricanes. Hurricanes only form when sea surface temperatures reach 80°F or higher. When this warm water evaporates, the vapor rises, forming tall towers of cumulus clouds and triggering rain. The rain releases heat energy, warming the air and further lowering the air pressure. As air rises to fill this low pressure trough, even more moist air is drawn up from the ocean and a self-feeding, self-propelling energy engine is created.

Hurricanes develop above and below the Equator, but only between 5 and 30 degrees latitude, where the Coriolis force can kick in and make the warm, moist air that flows into the low pressure trough spin. Inside the eye, the area of very low pressure from 5 to 100 miles wide at the center of the storm, winds are light and the weather is fair. The most violent activity, rain and turbulent winds, takes place in the towering wall of clouds surrounding the eye: the eye wall. The trade winds, and the winds generated by the storm itself, propel the storm forward. When the wind speed in a tropical cyclone reaches 38 miles an hour, it becomes a tropical

wires, communication was cut off. Galvestonians were accustomed to high waves, and most of the houses near the beach were built on stilts. Instead of heeding the warnings, many residents gathered on the beach to watch the huge waves, which ballooned higher than 15 feet. Winds clocked at 130 miles an hour pummeled the coast, and atmospheric pressure plummeted. Bridges to the mainland were knocked out, preventing evacuation. As the storm progressed, many residents fled to the highest point in the city—only 8.7 feet above sea level—but the relentless waters soon reached them.

"QUEEN OF THE WAVES"

St. Mary's Orphan Asylum, operated by the Sisters of Charity to care for children who had lost their parents during yellow fever epidemics, was housed in two two-story buildings just beyond the dunes, with balconies facing the Gulf. Attempting to calm the children by having them sing an old French hymn, "Queen of the Waves," the nuns gathered all the orphans on the top floor of the girls' dormitory. Using clothesline, each nun tied six or eight children to the cincture she wore around her waist. But the storm ripped the building off its foundation, and the roof came crashing down. All ten of the nuns perished, along with

Survivors of the hurricane that destroyed one-third of Galveston, Texas, in 1900 sift through the ruins of a church. In the wake of the hurricane, looting was widespread, and at least 125 looters were shot.

90 children. Only three boys survived, clinging to a floating tree until it washed ashore.

In the aftermath of the storm, chaos, crime, and kindness contended. Hot, humid weather rendered the stench from human and animal corpses unbearable. At first, weights were tied to the bodies and they were pushed out to sea, but the sea kept returning them. Then, they were burned in makeshift funeral pyres—but not before looters attempted to rob the dead. Martial law was established, and at least 125 looters were executed. Relief workers flocked to the city, including American Red Cross founder Clara Barton, who personally delivered food and medical supplies to the survivors. Barton also introduced a new cash crop, strawberry plants, to a farming community near Galveston that had also been devastated by the hurricane.

This Category Four hurricane, which NOAA calls "the deadliest disaster in American history," changed Galveston forever. The once bustling port city that boosters had touted as "a second Chicago" was instead relegated to the role of a beach town for nearby Houston.

Could a disaster of this magnitude happen today?

According to NOAA, "it's possible. Even though there have been great technological advances in weather forecasting in the past 100 years and the city has erected an 18-foot seawall, Galveston is not invincible to such powerful storms. Since many people in the

A victim of the Galveston, Texas, hurricane of 1900 is consigned to a funeral pyre. More than 8,000 people perished in what Galvestonians still refer to simply as "the storm."

United States have moved closer to the shore, trying to evacuate the population of Galveston could take days."

TRAGEDY IN BANGLADESH

Low-lying coastal areas with large populations are at high risk for hurricane disasters. Some 11 million people live along the river-laced coast of the Bay of Bengal in Bangladesh, in crowded communities and on offshore islands. In November 1970, a tropical cyclone swept across the Bay of Bengal. Winds of more than 100 miles an hour and 30-foot waves devastated the area, causing mammoth flooding and leaving 300,000 to 500,000 dead—the highest toll in hurricane history. Although the area will always be prone to such storms, a preparedness program run by the government of Bangladesh and the Bangladesh Red Crescent Society may be increasing the coastal population's chances of surviving these natural disasters. The group has recruited volunteers to alert people to coming storms, and has built cyclone shelters. Thanks to such efforts, a severe cyclone that hit the area in 1994 saw only 127 deaths. Some 750,000 people were successfully evacuated.

Poverty is a strong risk factor for turning natural disasters into human tragedies. Poor countries usually lack the infrastructure needed to protect people from storms or to remove them from harm's way. The four major hurricanes that pummeled Florida in the fall of 2004, for example, inflicted major economic damage and disruption but killed fewer than a hundred people. In contrast, just one of those hurricanes—Jeanne—left more than 2,000 people dead in poverty-stricken Haiti.

IMPACT OF GLOBAL WARMING

Will global warming make hurricanes and cyclones worse?

In low-lying areas such as Bangladesh, the rising sea levels associated with climate change could certainly spell annihilation. And some scientists believe that increasing greenhouse gases that are triggering global warming will intensify hurricanes. Dr. Thomas R. Knutson of the NOAA/Geophysical Fluid Dynamics Laboratory and Dr. Robert F. Tuleya of Old Dominion University simulated hurricanes under warmer conditions with more carbon dioxide in the atmosphere and predicted that, by the 2080s, seas warmed by increasing carbon dioxide in the atmosphere, will increase hurricane strength an extra half step on the Saffir-Simpson Scale and make rainfall up to 60 miles from the core almost 20 percent more CONTINUED ON PAGE 172

Sweeping off the Bay of Bengal, a tropical cyclone rammed East Pakistan, now Bangladesh, in November 1970, destroying homes, obliterating whole villages, and killing more than 300,000 people.

ON THE OPPOSITE PAGE: According to scientists, thin, streaky clouds form around small particles in the exhaust of ships and planes. These clouds hold less moisture and cool the earth less than other clouds.

ON THE FOLLOWING PAGES: **Hurricane Andrew plows a path of destruction toward the East Coast of the United States in this time-lapse image showing the storm on August 23, 24, and 25, 1992.**

ON PAGES 170-171: **Seen from space on September 13, 2003, Hurricane Isabel's eye, the center of the hurricane, is relatively calm, the eye wall is a solid ring of thunderstorms, containing the storm's most violent weather.**

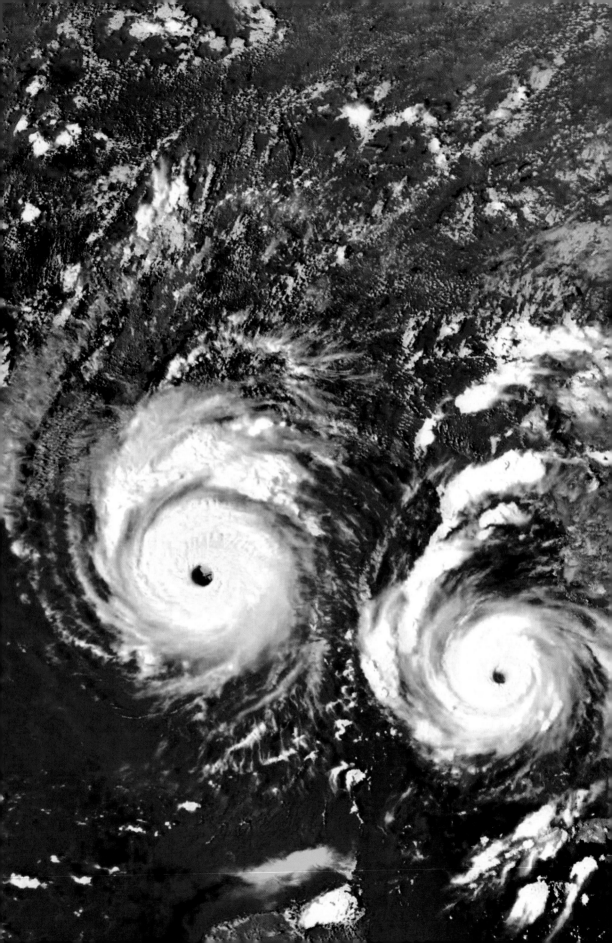

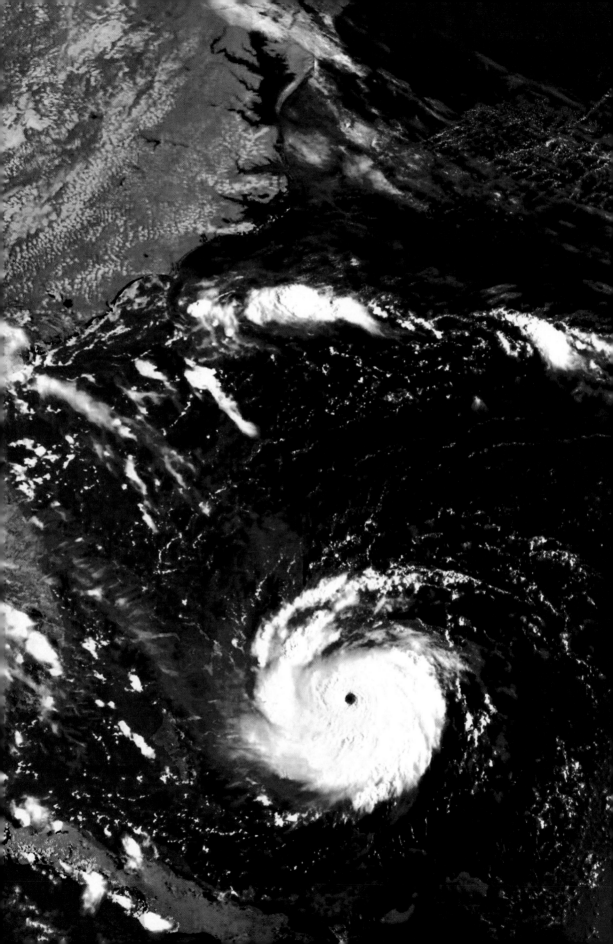

intense. Even if the number of hurricanes stays constant, the scientists wrote in the *Journal of Climate* in September 2004, the increased intensity would amplify the destructive power of these storms.

The El Niño-La Niña cycle also impacts hurricanes. During La Niña years in the United States, abnormally cool waters in the tropical Pacific mean colder winters in the Northwest and Midwest, less rain in the Gulf of Mexico and the Southeast, and drought in the Southwest. The westerly winds across the United States weaken, so tropical storms in the Atlantic meet little wind resistance and are more likely to strike land. According to one study, the probability of three or more major hurricanes in the Atlantic basin is four times more likely in a La Niña year than in an El Niño year. Conversely, El Niño conditions tend to increase the number of tropical storms in the Pacific.

PROJECT STORMFURY

During the 1960s and 1970s, NOAA and its predecessor agency tried to mitigate hurricanes by seeding clouds just outside the hurricane's eye wall with silver iodide, an ice nucleus. The government scientists seeded clouds during Hurricanes Esther (1961), Beulah (1963), Debbie (1969), and Ginger (1971). The ice nuclei were supposed to cause the supercooled waters in the clouds to freeze, enhancing the thunderstorms, liberating latent heat, and causing a rain band to form at the expense of the eye wall and weakening the winds at the hurricane's inner core.

Although the theory made meteorological sense, it didn't work in practice—in large part because most hurricanes don't have enough supercooled water for seeding to be effective. In addition, there was no sure way to tell whether the hurricanes that did weaken after seeding would not have done so naturally. At best, the results were inconclusive, and the project was discontinued.

FORECASTING HURRICANES

Today, the best defenses against hurricanes are considered to be prediction and preparation.

The National Hurricane Center in Miami, Florida, is "hurricane central" for the Atlantic coast, while a similar facility in Pearl Harbor, Hawaii, keeps watch over the Pacific and Indian Oceans. Meteorologists at these centers track tropical depressions, tropical storms, and tropical cyclones (hurricanes), and try to determine in advance where they will hit and how bad they will be.

Satellites orbiting the Earth about 22,000 miles above the Equator, provide forecasters with data about the location, size, and intensity of storms, and pictures of their surrounding environments. Land-based radar helps meteorologists monitor hurricanes as they approach land, and supplies information about winds. And daring pilots fly into the cores of hurri-

During the 1960s and 1970s, meteorologists tried, with only limited success, to prevent hurricanes by seeding thunderclouds with silver iodide to make them rain, thus weakening the eye wall.

canes to pinpoint the storm's center and to measure wind, pressure, temperature, and humidity.

These flights began in 1943, when flight instructor Joe Duckworth decided to prove the airworthiness of his small training plane by flying it into a hurricane off the Texas coast. Later, military pilots conducted airborne reconnaissance of Pacific typhoons, which were doing almost as much damage to the U.S. fleet as the Japanese were inflicting during the war. Today, planes collect data from inside storms and measure the winds driving hurricanes toward land.

The planes launch "dropwindsondes," instrument packages about the size of three beer cans, which track the storm's position, the rate of drift, the temperature, and atmospheric pressure. The data is radioed back every one and a half feet.

"It's the equivalent of a CT scan that tells us what the atmosphere is doing at various levels," said National Hurricane Center spokesman Frank Lepore.

In addition to the planes that fly right into hurricanes, NOAA's Gulf Stream IV, a high altitude jet, flies in the environment around hurricanes in order to better define the steering currents and determine where the storm is headed. CONTINUED ON PAGE 178

WHAT IS IT LIKE TO FLY INTO A HURRICANE?

According to National Hurricane Center spokesman Frank Lepore, it's "hours of tedium plus about half an hour when your stomach is turned inside out." But you can experience the flight without leaving terra firma by taking a "cyberflight" with the Hurricane Hunters of the 53rd Weather Reconnaissance Squadron. Go to www.hurricanehunters.com/cyberfly.htm. There's no risk, and at the end of the flight, you'll even get a squadron patch.

Data from reconnaissance flights, satellites, radar, and other sources is fed into computers at the National Hurricane Center, which uses several different models to help meteorologists forecast the path, speed, and strength of the storm; and the storm surge height and possible flooding. When a hurricane is predicted to hit within 36 hours, the National Hurricane Center issues a "hurricane watch." When sustained winds of 74 mph or more are expected within 24 hours, a "hurricane warning" is issued.

A U.S. Air Force plane laden with sensors stands ready to fly into severe weather to send back data about tropical storms and hurricanes to the National hurricane Center in Miami through a satellite link.

ON THE FOLLOWING PAGES: Pilots in the 53rd Weather Reconnaissance Squadron fly their C-130J plane into a developing storm. During a hurricane, crews fly round the clock, collecting data from inside the storm.

C

Vortex hits 80 mph. On the side where it spins with winds averaging 120 mph, it reaches 200 mph, ruining homes in mere seconds. On the side where it spins against surrounding winds, it slows to a benign 40 mph.

Intense updraft

B

Vortex stretches and increases to 40 mph, causing peak winds of 160 mph.

Intense updraft

ANDREW'S RECKLESS RIDE

The official warning came at 8 a.m., August 23, 1992. A full 21 hours later few were ready for what hit—the third-strongest hurricane to strike the U.S. mainland in the 20th century. Spawning winds that some scientists believe may have reached 200 miles an hour, Andrew caused $26.5 billion in damage. It became the nation's costliest natural disaster. But damage could have been worse. Andrew crossed Florida far to the south and raced at nearly 20 miles and hour, twice the usual pace for hurricanes in this region. Had the eye struck Miami and Fort Lauderdale, scores more might have died. Had it lingered, more wildlife might have perished. Such what-ifs prompt coastal dwellers to keep a cautious eye on the horizon.

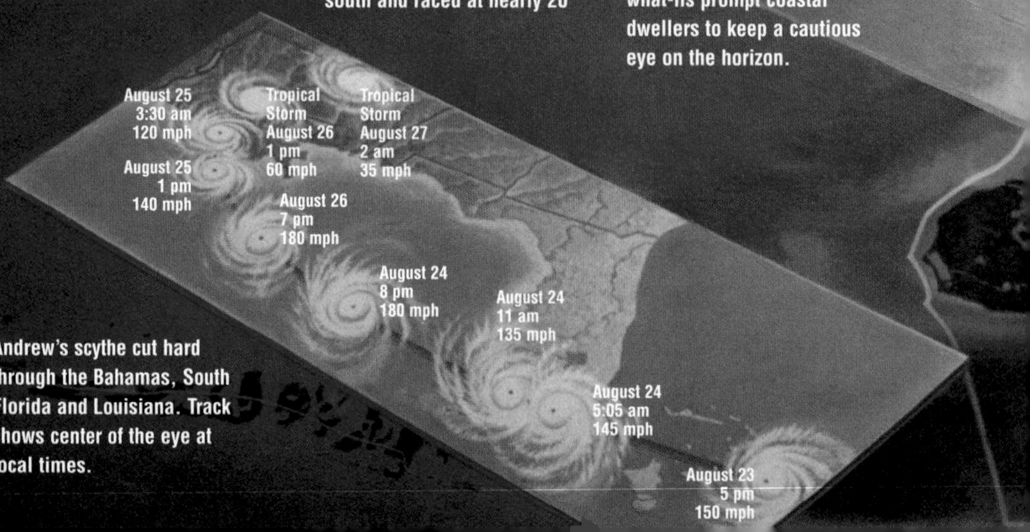

August 25
3:30 am
120 mph

Tropical Storm
August 26
1 pm
60 mph

Tropical Storm
August 27
2 am
35 mph

August 25
1 pm
140 mph

August 26
7 pm
180 mph

August 24
8 pm
180 mph

August 24
11 am
135 mph

August 24
5:05 am
145 mph

August 23
5 pm
150 mph

Andrew's scythe cut hard through the Bahamas, South Florida and Louisiana. Track shows center of the eye at local times.

Intense updraft

Vortex spinning at 20 mph and traveling with winds averaging 120 mph can create winds of 140 mph.

New theory of eyewall offspring

Vortices that whirl between winds of different speeds can be stretched by intense updrafts (A), says Ted Fujita, professor emeritus of the University of Chicago. Gaining speed as they stretch (B), the "spin-up vortices" can leave 50-to-300-foot-wide swaths of ruin (C).

The fiery inner eyewall

Currents of warm, moist air (purple arrows) spiral toward the voracious low-pressure eye. As the air rises, water vapor condenses, releasing heat that fuels hurricane winds. In Andrew, some updrafts raged with rare intensity, spawning destructive vortices beneath them.

Center of eye

Hit by the peak storm surge of 10.9 feet, Burger King headquarters was nearly gutted.

The National Hurricane Center lost its radar and anemometer, which recorded a top gust of 164 mph.

Miccosukee Indian Reservation

In the Everglades, 70,000 acres of mangroves were destroyed. Nonnative trees may replace them.

At Turkey Point power plant a smokestack was lost but nuclear reactors were unharmed.

• Fort Lauderdale

Coral Gables

• Miami

Homestead Air Force Base was leveled. Its annual payroll had put 144 billion dollars into south Dade's pockets.

Scouring currents ripped apart sea fans, sponges, and coral in areas of Biscayne Bay.

Florida's painful scar

With its fiercest winds spanning some 25 miles, Andrew sliced across 60 miles of Florida, felling orchards, grinding houses to mulch and denuding hardwood hammocks.

How dangerous is it to fly into or around a hurricane? Since 1944, four planes with a total of 36 persons aboard have been lost to storms.

HOW ACCURATE ARE THESE FORECASTS?

In assessing the accuracy of hurricane forecasts, meteorologists look at two measures: track and intensity, where the hurricane is going and how strong it will be. According to Frank Lepore of the National Hurricane Center, between 1994 and 2003 the average error in forecasting the track of a hurricane 24 hours in advance, the time at which a hurricane warning would be issued, was 76 nautical miles. In contrast, the average error between 1964 and 1973 was 118 nautical miles.

"It's a process of continuous improvement," said Lepore. "We have better surveillance technology, and we're always improving numerical computer models. As for intensity, that's a less mature science. We're usually off by about 25 miles an hour at five days out. That's why we're investing money in intensity issues—in research on the dynamics of hurricanes."

INTERCEPTING HURRICANES

One way to find out about the dynamics of hurricanes is to drive into them with mobile truck-mounted Doppler radars. Dr. Joshua Wurman of the Center for Severe Weather Research in Boulder, Colorado, has intercepted eight hurricanes, beginning with Hurricane Fran in 1996.

"We take two or three trucks and meet at the coast days ahead of the storm," he said. "With Hurricane Frances, in 2004, we took the trucks to a central place in Florida—Orlando—and then headed for Fort Pierce. We try to target the right eye wall—the worst part of the storm. We look for an exposed place, with no trees or blockage in the way, as close to the shore as we can get without being flooded. We also try not to park downstream from a

building we think may be blown apart. There's a lot of tedium and a lot of talking. We have to talk people into letting us park our trucks on their property. We have to convince them we're not crazies. When the storm starts, we're in very nasty winds, and we're stuck in the truck for eight to ten hours. One man tried to get out to go to the bathroom, and the winds ripped the door off the truck."

These Doppler on Wheels expeditions have made an important contribution to hurricane research: the discovery of intense rolls in the winds of

Radar shows Hurricane Hugo spinning toward landfall near Charleston, South Carolina, on September 22, 1989. Hugo, which began near the Cape Verde Islands, inflicted damages estimated at $7 billion.

A Doppler on Wheels heads toward a rendezvous with
raging weather. Driven into hurricanes and tornadoes,
these mobile units rake the skies with radar beams,
collecting data from inside the spinning storms.

the boundary layer, the layer of air closest to the Earth's surface.

"In a hurricane, the wind blows at different speeds—it oscillates," explains Dr. Wurman. "We found that the wind, instead of going straight, is going in a corkscrew pattern. And the part coming down is bringing the fastest air in the hurricane from aloft to the ground, where it can do the most damage."

Scientists such as Dr. Wurman can intercept hurricanes and use Doppler radar to find out more about what makes them tick. Hurricane Hunter planes can fly into hurricanes and track their positions and measure their intensity. Satellites can orbit the Earth and send back pictures of brewing hurricanes. Continuing improvements in forecasting can reduce the deaths and damages caused by hurricanes. But hurricanes will remain one of nature's most powerful forces—a violent cacophony of wind, waves, and rain that may, in time, be better understood but that will never, ever be tamed.

WHAT'S IN A NAME?

Since 1950, hurricanes have been tagged with human names. This was done mainly for convenience, since it was easier for meteorologists to refer to "Hurricane Bob," for example, than to talk about "the hurricane that's closing in on the east coast of Barbados." Not only was the latter a more cumbersome term, but hurricanes move so fast that the original term quickly became inaccurate. At first, hurricanes were given only female names. Since 1979, however, alternating male and female names have been used, and Spanish and French names have been added. Six lists of names are used in rotation. Here are the names for upcoming Atlantic hurricanes.

2005 *Arlene, Bret, Cindy, Dennis, Emily, Franklin, Gert, Harvey, Irene, Jose, Katrina, Lee, Maria, Nate, Ophelia, Philippe, Rita, Stan, Tammy, Vince, and Wilma.*

2006 *Alberto, Beryl, Chris, Debby, Ernesto, Florence, Gordon, Helene, Isaac, Joyce, Kirk, Leslie, Michael, Nadine, Oscar, Patty, Rafael, Sandy, Tony, Valerie, and William.*

2007 *Andrea, Barry, Chantal, Dean, Erin, Felix, Gabrielle, Humberto, Ingrid, Jerry, Karen, Lorenzo, Melissa, Noel, Olga, Pablo, Rebekah, Sebastien, Tanya, Van, and Wendy.*

2008 *Arthur, Bertha, Cristobal, Dolly, Edouard, Fay, Gustav, Hanna, Ike, Josephine, Kyle, Laura, Marco, Nana, Omar, Paloma, Rene, Sally, Teddy, Vicky, and Wilfred.*

2009 *Ana, Bill, Claudette, Danny, Erika, Fred, Grace, Henri, Ida, Joaquin, Kate, Larry, Mindy, Nicholas, Odette, Peter, Rose, Sam, Teresa, Victor, and Wanda.*

2010 *Alex, Bonnie, Charley, Danielle, Earl, Frances, Gaston, Hermine, Ivan, Jeanne, Karl, Lisa, Matthew, Nicole, Otto, Paula, Richard, Shary, Tomas, Virginie, and Walter.*

For lists of names of tropical cyclones in other parts of the world, go to www.nhc.noaa.gov/aboutnames.shtml.

A satellite image captured Hurricane Linda approaching
Baja California on September 12, 1997. Linda generat-
ed wind gusts up to 220 miles an hour off the coast of
Mexico, but weakened over cooler waters to the north.

NOAA'S TOP GLOBAL WEATHER/CLIMATE EVENTS OF THE 20TH CENTURY

Asian Droughts	India, 1900, 1907, 1965-67; China, 1907, 1928-30, 1936, 1941-42; Soviet Union 1921-22
Sahel Drought	1910-14, 1940-44, 1970-85
China Typhoons	1912, 1922
Yangtze River Flood	1931
Great Smog of London	1952
Europe Storm Surge	1953
Great Iran Flood	1954
Typhoon Vera, Japan	1958
Bangladesh Cyclones	1970, 1991
North Vietnam Flood	1971
Iran Blizzard	1972
El Niño	1982-83
Typhoon Thelma, Philippines	1991
Hurricane Mitch, Honduras and Nicaragua	1998

SAMPLER OF WEATHER PROVERBS

Hark! I hear the asses bray, we shall have some rain today.
Clear moon, frost soon.
When the deer are in gray coat in October, expect a severe winter.
If salt is sticky and gains in weight, it will rain before too late.
Dandelion blossoms close before a rain.
When smoke rises, but not too high, clouds won't grow, and you'll keep dry.
A warm Christmas, a cold Easter.
If wasps build their nests high, the winter will be long and harsh.
It will be a cold, snowy winter if the breastbone of a fresh-cooked turkey is dark purple.
If the goose honks high, fair weather; if the goose honks low, foul weather.
If the bull leads the cows to pasture, expect rain; if the cows precede the bull, the weather will be uncertain.

CHRONOLOGY
OF WEATHER
INVENTIONS

1450	Italian architect Leon Battista Alberti invents the first mechanical anemometer, a device to measure the speed of wind.
1608	Italian physicist and mathematician Evangelista Torricelli invents the barometer. In order to do vacuum experiments, Torricelli, an assistant to Galileo, filled a four-foot-long glass tube with mercury and inverted the tube into a dish. Some of the mercury stayed in the tube. Torricelli discovered that the height of the mercury varied from day to day depending on the atmospheric pressure.
1662	British architect Christopher Wren invents the tipping bucket rain gauge to measure precipitation. Earlier, King Sejong of Korea had used a calibrated cylinder to measure rain.
1714	German physicist Gabriel Fahrenheit invents the mercury thermometer and introduces the temperature scale that bears his name.
1742	Swedish astronomer Anders Celsius devises the Celsius, or centigrade, temperature scale.
1842	Austrian mathematician Christian Doppler discovers that sound waves can be used to measure speed and distance. His principles are the basis of radar systems that help meteorologists measure wind speeds and determine where and how fast air masses are moving.
1844	Samuel F. B. Morse invents the telegraph, making it possible to rapidly communicate weather news.
1940s	During World War II, radar is invented, and military pilots discover the jet stream.
1950s	First computer models to help analyze and forecast weather developed.
1960	First weather satellite put into orbit.

HOW TO READ A WEATHER MAP

Red line with scallops = WARM FRONT. Air will probably become warmer and more humid than it was before.

Blue line with pointed triangles = COLD FRONT. As the cold front passes, temperatures will drop, pressure will rise, and showers may occur, followed by clearing.

Alternating blue and red lines with blue triangles pointing toward warmer air and red scallops pointing toward colder air = STATIONARY FRONT, one that isn't moving. Wind shift and temperature changes on either side of the front.

Purple line with scallops and triangles = OCCLUDED FRONT. This occurs when a cold front catches up to a warm front. As the front passes, pressure usually rises and light to moderate precipitation, followed by clearing, may occur.

H = HIGH PRESSURE ZONE. Descending air will warm and bring fair weather.

L = LOW PRESSURE ZONE. Rising air will cool and may bring clouds and rain.

Isobars are lines drawn on the map connecting points of identical pressure, while isotherms connect points of identical temperature.

Advection fog – Visible condensation caused by the horizontal movement of mild, humid air over a cold surface, such as the ocean.

Alberta Clipper – A fast moving storm that forms in the Province of Alberta, Canada, east of the Rockies.

Anemometer – A device used to measure the speed of wind.

Atmosphere – An envelope of air laden with moisture and bound to Earth by gravity.

Atmospheric pressure – The weight of air pressing down on the Earth's surface.

Baguios – A tropical cyclone in the seas surrounding Indonesia and the Philippines.

Barometer – An instrument that measures atmospheric pressure, usually by means of a column of mercury in a tube.

Blizzard – According to the National Weather Service, a blizzard includes falling or blowing snow accompanied by winds of 35 miles an hour or more, making for visibility of less than a quarter mile for an extended period.

Boundary layer – The layer of air closest to Earth, up to about a mile above the surface. In this layer, winds are affected by friction with the Earth's surface.

Climate – The average weather in a particular place or region over a time frame of about 30 years.

Contrails – Condensation trails formed from the vapor spewed into the atmosphere from high-altitude jet planes. The cold temperatures in the upper atmosphere turn the vapor into ice crystals that look like cirrus clouds.

Convergence – An atmospheric condition in which air flows into a region.

Coriolis force – A force stemming from the Earth's rotation that deflects air to the right in the Northern Hemisphere and to the left in the Southern Hemisphere.

Cumulus clouds – From the Latin word for "heap," these lumpy towers of clouds are usually found at lower levels.

Cirrus clouds – From the Latin word for "curl," cirrus clouds are wispy clouds found high in the atmosphere.

Dew – Water vapor that condenses on grass, flowers, plants, and other objects near the ground during a cool but above-freezing night.

Dew point – The temperature at which water vapor in a given parcel of air condenses.

Doldrums – An area of calm right near the Equator where the northeast and southwest trade winds meet.

Easterly wave – A wave-like disturbance in a tropical region that moves from east to west and may eventually trigger a tropical cyclone.

El Niño – The periodic warming of ocean waters off the Pacific coast of South America that can significantly change weather patterns in the United States.

Ensemble forecasting – A method of forecasting in which a collection of forecasts is generated by computer models with varying inputs in an attempt to improve accuracy.

Eye – An area of very low pressure from 5 to 100 miles wide at the center of a tropical cyclone.

Eye wall – A towering wall of clouds surrounding the eye of a tropical cyclone.

Flash floods – Fast moving floods that occur within six hours of a rain storm, a dam or levee failure, or the sudden release of water by an ice jam.

Foehn winds – Warm, dry winds, such as the Chinook in the Rocky Mountains, zonda winds in Argentina, the No'wester in New Zealand, the hamsin in the Middle East, the Diablo winds around San Francisco, and the Santa Ana winds in southern California.

Fog – According to the American Meteorological Society, fog is "a visible aggregate of minute water droplets suspended in the atmosphere near the Earth's surface." In other words, it's a cloud on or near the ground.

Fronts – The leading edges of air masses of different temperatures.

Frost – Water vapor that forms on a surface colder than the surrounding air and that has a temperature below freezing.

Freezing rain – Rain that freezes on impact, coating the ground or other objects with ice.

Glory – Rings of color produced by water droplets in clouds and fog that break up the sun's light and bend it around a shadow. Glories are sometimes seen ringing the shadow of an airplane on the clouds.

Greenhouse effect – The phenomenon of gases in the atmosphere, mainly water vapor and carbon dioxide, trapping part of the Earth's heat and preventing it from escaping into space.

Gustnado – A whirlwind that forms in the outflow of a thunderstorm. Gustnadoes are sometimes mistaken for tornadoes.

Haboob – A strong wind that creates sand storms in the Sudan.

Hail – Precipitation in the form of lumps of ice.

Halo – A ring around the sun or moon caused by light shining through thin cirrus or cirrostratus clouds.

Horse latitudes – An area of calm at about 30 degrees latitude where the trade winds meet the prevailing westerlies. Reportedly, sailing ships delayed by the lack of wind sometimes had to throw cargo horses overboard here to conserve water.

Humboldt Current – A cold current surrounded by warming waters in the Pacific Ocean off Peru

Hurricane – The Carib Indian-derived name for a tropical cyclone that forms in the Atlantic or Caribbean. A tropical storm becomes a hurricane when it gains wind speeds of 74 miles an hour or higher.

Isobar – A line drawn on a weather map to connect points of equal pressure.

Jet streak – A bundle of strong winds within a jet stream.

Jet stream – A fast, undulating river of wind about five miles above Earth.

Katabatic winds – From a Greek word meaning "going downhill," a wind that blows down a mountain, hill or glacier.

Lake-effect snow – Snow that falls on the lee side of large lakes, where clouds drop the moisture they have acquired passing over the body of water.

La Niña – The periodic cooling of ocean temperatures off the Pacific coast of South America that can bring changes in the weather patterns of the United States.

Mean Heat Index – The average of the temperatures during the hottest and coolest part of a day.

Mesosphere – The layer of the atmosphere from about 30 to 50 miles above the Earth's surface.

Meteorology – Science that deals with the study of the atmosphere and of weather.

Microburst wind shear – Violent downward air blasts that can cause airplanes to lose lift and crash.

Mistral – A cold katabatic wind that flows down from the Massif Central and the Pyrenees in France and brings cold, windy weather to the Mediterranean coast.

Monsoon – From the Arabic word for seasons, a wind that changes with the seasons, notably in India and Southeast Asia.

Moonbows – Lunar rainbows. When moonlight hits drops of rain, the raindrop acts like a prism and separates the light into the colors of the spectrum. Because of the lower light at night, moonbows usually appear as all-white light.

Nimbus clouds – From the Latin word for rain, nimbus clouds are clouds that generate rain.

Noctilucent clouds – Night-luminous clouds that develop about 50 miles above Earth and can be seen in the higher latitudes.

Nor'easter – A cyclonic storm that forms on the east coast of North America, usually between September and April.

Norther – A strong, cold northerly wind that sweeps across the southern plains as far south as Texas; sometimes called a Blue Norther.

Papagayo – A violent northeasterly wind that strikes the Pacific coast of Central America in the fall.

Peru Current – See Humboldt Current.

Pineapple Express – A southwest wind that brings warm, humid air and often heavy rain to the Pacific Northwest and California.

Polar high – High pressure ridge at about 90° north and south latitude.

Polar jet stream – Fast river of wind about five miles above the Earth at mid-latitudes, flowing from west to east at about 60 to 95 miles an hour.

Pressure gradient force – The difference in atmospheric pressure between air masses. The pressure gradient force pushes air from areas of high pressure to areas of low pressure, creating wind.

Radiant energy – Energy from the sun, moving in waves.

Radiation fog – Ground fog, the most common kind of fog. It forms when the ground cools and causes condensation in the layers of air nearest the Earth.

Rayleigh scattering – The principle, named for the English physicist who discovered it, that the gas molecules in the atmosphere scatter the violet and blue colors of the spectrum move effectively than the other colors.

Ridge – An area of high atmospheric pressure.

Sahel – A broad band cutting across Africa just south of the Sahara.

Shamal – A wind that blows northwesterly over Iraq and the Persian Gulf in summer.

Sirocco – A hot, dry wind from the Sahara that brings storms to the Mediterranean and cold, wet weather to Europe. Also called the scirocco or the jugo.

Sleet – Precipitation formed when ice crystals melt partially on their way to Earth and then refreeze.

Smog – A combination of fog and smoke or other pollutants

Snowstorm – According to the National Weather Service, a snowstorm entails six inches of heavy snow, ice accumulation, and dangerous wind chills.

Squall – A sharp increase in wind speed, about 16 knots or at least three steps on the Beaufort Scale, lasting about a minute, often along a cold front.

Squamish – A cold polar wind that funnels into fjords in British Columbia.

Storm cell – The smallest unit of a storm-producing system; an air mass that contains up and down drafts in convective loops.

Stratus clouds – From the Latin word for layer, stratus clouds develop in layers wider than they are thick and tend to cover most of the sky.

Sun dogs – So called because they stick close to their master, sundogs are bright, multicolored patches of light on both sides of the sun. Sometimes called "mock suns," they are caused by sunlight passing through ice crystals inside clouds.

Sunspots – Relatively cool areas of the sun that appear as dark blotches. The relationship between sunspots and weather on Earth is controversial.

Supercooled water – Water that's cooled to below-freezing temperatures, yet remains liquid.

Thermals – Bubbles of hot air that rise upward in the atmosphere, cooling as they rise.

Tornado – A violent wind storm created by a spiraling column of air that extends down from a cumulonimbus cloud.

Trade winds – Persistent winds that blow from east to west in the area between the Equator and 30 degrees latitude.

Tropical cyclone – An area of low pressure in tropical latitudes around which winds flow counterclockwise in the Northern Hemisphere and clockwise in the Southern Hemisphere.

Tropical depression – A circulating weather system over tropical waters with wind speeds between 25 to 38 miles an hour.

Tropical storm – A tropical depression that has gained wind speeds of 39 to 73 miles an hour

Tropopause – The top of the troposphere.

Troposphere – The lowest level of the atmosphere, where most of our weather occurs.

Trough – An area of low atmospheric pressure.

Typhoon – A tropical cyclone in the Pacific.

Upslope fog – Visible condensation formed when winds blow moist air upward over higher terrain.

Waterspout – A weak tornado that develops over water.

Weather – According to the American Meteorological Society, weather is "the state of the atmosphere, mainly with respect to its effect upon life and human activities at a particular time, as defined by various weather elements," such as temperature, humidity, and precipitation.

Williwaw – A wind that blasts down the mountains to the sea in the Aleutians or the Straits of Magellan.

Willy-willy – The Australian name for a tropical cyclone

Wind Chill Index – A table that combines temperature and wind speed to indicate the combined effect on the human body.

Wind shear – A sudden and drastic change in wind direction over a short distance.

Agnone, John G., ed., *Raging Forces: Earth in Upheaval,* Washington, DC, National Geographic Society, 1995
Allaby, Michael, *Hurricanes,* New York, NY, Facts on File, Inc., 1997
Allen, Oliver E., *Atmosphere,* Alexandria, VA, Time-Life Books, 1983
Davies, Pete, *Inside the Hurricane,* New York, NY, Henry Holt and Co., 2000
Davis, Devra, "The Great Smog," *History Today,* Vol. 52, No. 12, p.2, December 1, 2002
Dickinson, Michael J. et al, "The March 1993 Superstorm Cyclogenesis: Incipient Phase Synoptic- and Convective-Scale Flow Interaction and Model Performance," *Monthly Weather Review,* Vol. 125, December 1997, pp. 3041-3072
Doswell III, Charles A. et al., "Storm Spotting and Public Awareness Since the First Tornado Forecasts of 1948," *Weather and Forecasting,* Vol. 14, No. 4, pp. 544-557
Durschmied, Erik, *The Weather Factor: How Nature Has Changed History,* Arcade Books, 2002
Eckardt, Frank D. and Robert S. Schemenauer, "Fog water chemistry in the Namib Desert, Namibia," *Atmospheric Environment,* Vol. 32, Issues 14-15, August 1998, pp. 2595-2599
Grazulis, Thomas P., *The Tornado: Nature's Ultimate Windstorm,* Norman, OK, University of Oklahoma Press, 2001
Greer, Ira, ed., *Glossary of Weather and Climate,* American Meteorological Society, 1996
Hall, James P., *Exploring and Understanding Weather and Climate,* Winchester, IL, Benefic Press, 1970
Harden, Blaine, "BRRR!: Whenever the Snow and Chill Get You Down This Winter, Remember the Winter of '99, When Only Millionaires Were Warm and Snow Drifted Six Feet Deep," *Washington Post Magazine,* December 27, 1981, p. 9
Hodgson, Michael, *Weather Forecasting,* Guilford, CT, The Globe Pequot Press, 1999
Hoerling, Martin and Arun Kumar, "The Perfect Ocean for Drought," *Science,* Vol. 299, Issue 5607, January 31, 2003, pp. 691-694
Knight, Nancy C., "No Two Alike?", *Bulletin of the American Meteorological Society,* Vol. 69, No. 5, May 1988, p.496
Knutson, Thomas R., and Robert E. Tuleya, "Impact of CO2-Induced Warming on Simulated Hurricane Intensity and Precipitation: Sensitivity to the Choice of Climate Model and Convective Parameterization," *Journal of Climate,* Vol.17, No.18, September 15, 2004, pp. 3477-3495
Larrain, H. et al., "Fog measurements at the site 'Falda Verde' north of Chanaral compared with other fog stations of Chile," *Atmospheric Research,* Vol. 64, Issues 1-4, September-October 2002, pp. 273-284
Larson, Erik, *Isaac's Storm,* New York, NY, Vintage Books, 2000
Lawrence, Bonnie S., ed., *Restless Earth,* Washington, DC, National Geographic Society, 1997
Nash, J. Madeleine, *El Niño,* New York, NY, Warner Books, Inc., 2002
National Geographic Society, "Global Warming: Bulletins From a Warmer World," *National Geographic,* September, 2004
Schubert, Siegfried D. et al., "On the Cause of the 1930s Dust Bowl," *Science,* Vol. 303, Issue 5665, March 19, 2004, pp. 1855-1859 Stott, Peter A., D. A. Stone, and M. R. Allen, "Human contribution to the European heatwave of 2003," *Nature,* 432, December 2, 2004, pp. 610-614
Toomey, David, *Stormchasers,* New York, NY, W.W. Norton & Company, 2002
Wurman, Joshua and Jennifer Winslow, "Intense Sub-Kilometer Scale Boundary Layer Rolls Observed in Hurricane Fran," *Science,* Vol. 280, April 24, 1998, p.555
Young, Andrew T., "Sunset science. III. Visual adaptation and green flashes," *Journal of the Optical Society of America,* Vol. 17, December 2000, pp. 2129-2139

PHOTO CREDITS

Pgs. 2-3 Michael S. Yanashita; pgs. 4-5 Michael S. Yamashita; pgs. 6-7 Michael S. Yamashuta; pg. 10 WarrenFaidley/Weatherstock; pg. 12 Earth Sciences and Image Analysis Laboratory at Johnson Space Center; pg. 14 Koji Nakamura; pgs. 16-17 Carter Kevin/Corbis Sygma; pgs 18-19 Reunion des Musees Nationaux/Art Resource; pgs. 20-21 Image Analysis Laboratory, NASA Johnson Space Center; pg. 22 Jim Brandenberg; pg. 23 Warren Faidley/Weather Stock; pgs. 24-25 Warren Faidley/Weather Stock pg. 26 Up Bettmann/CORBIS; pg. 26 Lo Farmer's Almanac/ Yankee Publishing Inc; pg. 27 NASA animation of Aura satellite by Jesse Allen and Reto Stöckli, Earth Observatory; pgs. 28-29 Jim Reed/ Corbis; pgs. 30-31 University Corporation for Atmospheric Research/NSF/Department of Energy; pgs. 32-33 NOAA in Space Collection; pgs. 34-35 Image courtesy Jacques Descloitres, MODIS Land Rapid Response Team; pg. 36 R. Ian Lloyd; pg. 38 Reto Stockli and Robert Simmon, NASA's Earth Observatory Team; pg. 39 Thomas Coax/AFP/Getty Images; pg. 40 NASA/Cathy Clerbaux, NCAR Atmospheric Chemistry Division; pg. 41 Peter Essick; pgs. 42-43 Michael Nichols; pgs. 44-45 NASA; pg. 46 Reuters/Corbis; pg. 47 Retuers/Corbis; pg. 48 AFP/Getty Images; pgs. 48-49 Library of Congress; pgs. 50-51 Library of Congress; pgs. 52-53 Layne Kennedy; pg. 55 Up and Lo Warren Faidley/Weatherstock; pg. 56 James P. Blair; pgs. 58-59 National Geographic Society Art; pg. 60 Up and Lo Warren Faidley/Weatherstock; pg. 61 Up and Lo Warren Faidley/Weatherstock; pgs. 62-63 University Corporation for Atmospheric Research, Photo by Carlye Calvin; pgs. 64-65 NASA Langley Research Center; pgs. 66-67 James P. Blair; pgs. 68-69 Getty Images; pg. 69 David Gordon Green; pgs. 72-73 James P. Blair; pgs. 74-75 Warren Faidley/Weatherstock; pgs. 76-77 Peter Essick; pgs. 78-79 George D. Lepp/Corbis; pgs. 80-81 Norbert Rosing; pgs. 82-83 Northwest Territories, Sage Suzuki; pg. 84 Randy Olson; pgs. 86-87 Bob Sasha; pgs. 88-89 Bob Sasha; pgs. 90-91 St Paul Pioneer Press/Corbis Sygma; pgs. 92-93 St Louis Post/Corbis Sygma; pgs. 94-95 AP /World Wide Photo; pgs. 96-96 Library of Congress; pgs. 98-99 Library of Congress; pgs. 100-101 Steve McCurry; pg. 103 Tom Murphy; pg. 104 Jericho Historical Society/snowflake bentley.com; pgs. 106-107 Reuters/Corbis; pgs. 108-109 MODIS Rapid Response Project at NASA/GSFC; pg. 110 Library of Congress; pg. 111 Bettmann/Corbis; pg. 113 NASA/NOAA; pg. 114 Norbert Rosing; pg. 116 National Geographic Society Maps; pgs. 118-119 Warren Faidley/Weatherstock; pg. 120-121 James P. Blair; pgs. 122-123 Warren Faidley/Weatherstock; pg. 125 Image Analysis Laboratory, NASA Johnson Space Center; pgs. 126-127 Reza; pgs. 128-129 EarlCryer/ZUMA/Corbis; pg. 131 Up Sandy Felsenthal; pg. 131 Sandy Felsenthal; pg. 132 Warren Faidley/Weatherstock; pg. 134 Warren Faidley/Weatherstock; pg. 137 Warren Faidley/Weatherstock; pg. 138 University Corporation for Atmospheric Research; pgs. 138-139 Warren Faidley/Weatherstock; pgs. 140-141 Warren Faidley/Weatherstock; pgs. 142-143 Warren Faidley/Weatherstock; pgs. 144-145 Ted Soqui/Corbis Sygma; pgs. 146-147 National Geographic Society Art; pg. 149 : Raymond J. Lustig, jr. pg. 151 National Center for Atmospheric Research; pg. 152 Carsten Peter; pg. 154 Richard R. Waite/ Corbis; pg. 156 Corbis; pg. 159 Warren Faidley/Weatherstock; pgs. 160-161 David S. Boyer; pgs. 162-163 Library of Congress; pg. 164 Library of Congress pg. 165 Library of Congress; pg. 166 Bettmann/Corbis; pg. 167 Jacques Descloitres, MODIS Land Rapid Response Team and Mark Gray, MODIS Atmosphere Science Team; pgs. 168-169 MODIS Rapid Response Project at NASA/GSFC; pgs. 170-171 Image courtesy of the Image Analysis Laboratory, NASA Johnson Space Center; pg. 172 Bill Curtsinger; pg. 173 Tech. Sgt. James B. Pritchett, 403rd Wing, United States Air Force; pgs. 174-175 Tech. Sgt. James B. Pritchett, 403rd Wing, United States Air Force; pgs. 176-177 National Geographic Society Art; pg. 178 Warren Faidley/Weatherstock; pg. 179 Warren Faidley/Weatherstock; pg. 181 NASA/Images and rendering by Marit Jentoft-Nilsen.

WEATHER: NATURE IN MOTION
By Anne H. Oman

Published by the National Geographic Society
John M. Fahey, Jr.,
President and Chief Executive Officer
Gilbert M. Grosvenor,
  Chairman of the Board
Nina D. Hoffman, *Executive Vice President
  and President of Books and Educational
  Publishing*

Prepared by the Book Division
Kevin Mulroy, *Senior Vice President
  and Publisher*
Kristin Hanneman, *Illustrations Director*
Marianne R. Koszorus, *Design Director*
Barbara Brownell Grogan, *Executive Editor*

Staff for this Book
Scott Mahler, *Project Editor*
Chris Anderson, *Illustrations Editor*
David M. Seager, *Art Director*
R. Gary Colbert, *Production Director*
Lewis Bassford, *Production Project Manager*
Rachel Sweeney, *Illustrations Specialist*
Dana Chivvis, *Illustrations Assistant*
Robert Swanson, *Indexer*

Manufacturing and Quality Control
Christopher A. Leidel, *Chief Financial Officer*
John T. Dunn, *Technical Director*
Clifford M. Brown, *Manager*
Phillip L. Schlosser, *Managing Director*

One of the world's largest nonprofit scientific and educational organizations, the National Geographic Society was founded in 1888 "for the increase and diffusion of geographic knowledge." Fulfilling this mission, the Society educates and inspires millions every day through its magazines, books, television programs, videos, maps and atlases, research grants, the National Geographic Bee, teacher workshops, and innovative classroom materials. The Society is supported through membership dues, charitable gifts, and income from the sale of its educational products. This support is vital to National Geographic's mission to increase global understanding and promote conservation of our planet through exploration, research, and education.

For more information, please call
1-800-NGS LINE (647-5463)
or write to the following address:

National Geographic Society
1145 17th Street N.W.
Washington, D.C. 20036-4688 U.S.A.

Visit the Society's Web site at
www.nationalgeographic.com.

Copyright © 2005 National Geographic Society.

All rights reserved. Reproduction of the whole or any part of the contents without permission is prohibited.

Printed in the U.S.A.

ISBN-0-7922-3815-X (Reg.)
ISBN: 0-7922-3816-8 (Deluxe)

Library of Congress Cataloging-in-Publication Data
Oman, Anne, 1940-
    Weather: nature in motion / Anne Oman.
      p. cm.
    Includes bibliographical references and index.
    ISBN 0-7922-3815-X (alk. paper)
      1. Weather--Popular works. 2. Weather--Pictorial works.
        I. Title.
    QC981.2.O43 2005
    551.6--dc22   2005047915